Fly
– on the –
Wall

Fly
– on the –
Wall

Recollections of Las Vegas' Good Old, Bad Old Days

DICK ODESSKY

Huntington Press Publishing
Las Vegas, Nevada

Fly on the Wall: Recollections of Las Vegas'
Good Old, Bad Old Days

Published by
Huntington Press
3687 South Procyon Avenue
Las Vegas, Nevada 89103
phone: (702) 252-0655
fax: (702) 252-0675
email: books@huntingtonpress.com

ISBN 0-929712-62-5

Cover Photo: Jason Cox
Cover Design: Jason Cox, Bethany Coffey Rihel
and Laurie Shaw
Interior Design and Production: Bethany Coffey Rihel
and Laurie Shaw

The hardcover edition of this book was published in 1999 by Huntington Press.

First paperback printing: April 2000

Photos accompanied by the following designations are courtesy of the University of Nevada-Las Vegas Library: Manis Collection, Las Vegas News Bureau, North Las Vegas Library Collection, Wilbur Clark Collection, and Sands Hotel Collection.

To Shirley "the Nag" LaMar, without whose constant prodding this book would never have become a reality. And to my wife Joyce, who has put up with me for more years than she might want to admit.

Acknowledgements

Deke Castleman: He wields a mean pencil, but his editing of *Fly on the Wall* definitely brought order out of chaos.

Anthony "Boss" Curtis: Our publisher and fearless leader, who doesn't mind going a round or two with his authors. I like to think we ended in a draw.

Jim Barrows: Another Las Vegas oldtimer, whose memory and files went a long way in keeping my facts straight. And Lynne Loomis, a stellar copy editor.

Benny Binion: Who contributed so much to the history of Las Vegas — and my liberal education.

M.B. "Moe" Dalitz: Who, with Benny Binion, was responsible for formulating Las Vegas and establishing "the book" by which the town operated.

Al Freeman and Eugene Murphy: Two of the brightest public-relations executives ever.

Ralph Lamb: Former Clark County Sheriff, who taught the residents of Clark County and the leaders of the legalized gaming industry how to live and work together.

Harley E. Harmon: For the masterful job he and his associates did in bringing harmony between the residents and the industry for so many years.

Morris Lansburgh: For teaching me — and Las Vegas — so much about operating a gaming resort and whose procedures are still valid throughout the international gaming industry.

General Harry Wald: For being such a splendid resort operator and a good friend.

Jay Sarno: Who brought pizzazz to Las Vegas with Caesars Palace and Circus Circus.

Michael and Jackie Gaughan: For being such good friends for so many years.

Howard Cannon: Former U.S. senator, who represented Nevada so well.

Peter Echeverria: The strongest and fairest chairman of the Nevada Gaming Commission I ever had the pleasure to know.

Glenn Neely: A gaming boss whose mold was broken just after he was born.

Sid Wyman and Carl Cohen: Two wonderful men and superb gaming operators, who watched over me during my tender years.

And Steve Delmont: My friend.

Table of Contents

Introduction

A Fly Is Born

Everything gets turned on its head in Las Vegas.

Back in the early 1950s, the people who ran the casino business found themselves in a strange position. These guys, who'd been criminals all their lives before migrating to southern Nevada, had become so comfortable operating within the law that now *they* had zero tolerance for crime. The word was out: Anyone breaking the law in Las Vegas had better hope he was caught by the police, because if "the boys" got to him first...well, you can figure out the rest.

Despite this unlikely transformation, the casino owners and executives were being besieged by an unfriendly press from all corners of the continent. It was a no-win situation. When they replied honestly to probing questions, their answers were twisted to fit the agendas of the reporters. When they realized they couldn't trust the press and began keeping their mouths shut, they were pilloried for hiding the truth.

My own position in the Las Vegas scheme of things was similarly topsy-turvy. I started out as a newspaperman, re-

porting on the events of the time. I was young and green
and in my glory. After all, these were Las Vegas' good old,
bad old days, and everyone in the world wanted to read
everything they could about what the nasty hoodlums who
ran the town were up to.

Rustling up the subject matter for compelling copy was
never a problem, but I knew one thing: I had to do everything possible to be honest and fair. I saw no reason to sen-
sationalize. Nor did I feel it was my place to report personal scandal. Truth is, I probably used less than 20 percent
of the information I gathered or that was fed to me.

I also refused to use a person's past against him. I knew
the criminal records of virtually everyone in the gambling
business, but I felt responsible for covering only their Las
Vegas activities. If they were able to come to Nevada and
convince the Gaming Control Board and Gaming Commission to license them, who was I to judge them further? I
now believe it was the way I handled those early confidences
that earned me the trust of the people who ran the Las Vegas show.

The boys liked talking to me. And as luck would have
it, I seemed always to be in a position to oblige them. I started
out working as a cub reporter at the *Las Vegas Sun* at the
tender age of 19, just after the grand opening of the Sahara
and the Sands took the town by storm. In 1960 I became the
youngest public-relations executive in Las Vegas when I
landed a job at the Flamingo. I stayed till 1967; I left while
the feds were busy putting many of my Flamingo bosses in
jail. In the '70s I worked as the marketing director at the
Stardust during the era glorified by the movie *Casino.* Then
I returned to the newspaper business, writing a six-day-a-
week column at the *Valley Times.*

My modus operandi — the switching back and forth between casino flack and newspaper hack — led many to won-

der about my motives. My writings at the *Valley Times* in particular—frequent condemnations of my former employers at the Stardust, which ultimately played a part in the demise of that dishonest operation—raised suspicions that I might have been a "mole" for federal agencies in their attempts to cleanse Las Vegas of its underworld influence. I've always found this suggestion laughable, since I'd also been accused of being a "cop hater" by one-time Los Angeles Chief of Police William Parker.

No, I was simply gravitating to where the action was— a habit that enabled me to become the proverbial fly on the wall during the most exciting quarter of a century in Las Vegas history.

1

Good Old Days

Sometime around 1830, a Mexican trader decided to try to find a shortcut off the Old Spanish Trail between Santa Fe and Los Angeles. Rumors that he was also looking for some loose slots to play to the contrary, his true motivation was in prolonging his life and the life of his horse.

Twenty miles or so from the last water hole, the trader was greeted by nothing but blazing hot sand, a few circling vultures, and — what was this? — a trickle of fresh water coming up out of the ground. He'd discovered one of many small springs, along with grass, trees, and even a creek, that existed, amazingly, in the middle of one of the harshest deserts on Earth. Little did he know that he stood near the spot that would one day be the heart of Glitter Gulch.

So far as is known, the trader never returned to build a home, a resort hotel, a themed restaurant, or even a 7-Eleven. He did, however, name the spring and the valley that surrounded it "Las Vegas," which in Spanish means "the Meadows."

For the next 70 years, Las Vegas was left to serve its purpose as the end of the world. One salient event occurred when the famous Western explorer and cartographer, John C. Fremont, stopped overnight by the springs in May 1844. His report to Congress on his surveys of the West was a national bestseller and created the impetus for the railroad builders who opened the frontier.

In fact, it was the San Pedro, Los Angeles and Salt Lake Railroad that, in the early 1900s, surveyed the valley area that the Mexican trader had found and determined it to be a fine stopping place for its steam locomotives en route from the coast to Salt Lake City.

In 1905, the railroaders staked out a town site, then held a big auction to sell off parcels of what would soon be the town of Las Vegas. Many of the parcels went unpurchased, but the railroad didn't mind. It hadn't paid much for the land to begin with. Las Vegas was now another railroad village.

From Burros to Bugsy

About the only strangers to pass through the area were some of the sourdough gold and silver miners, who were eking out a living prospecting the surrounding mountains. A poke of gold dust or a nugget or two meant mounting their burros and riding into town to sell their pickings; while there, they'd grab a bath, down some booze, and play some backroom faro. And though most of the townspeople were Mormons, whose religion forbade them from partaking in the vices, nothing prevented them from *taxing* the vices to help pay for improvements to the town.

Things didn't start to get serious in Las Vegas till 1930, when the U.S. government decided it was time to make use of the billions of gallons of water that flowed from the far-off Rocky Mountains, through the vast Western deserts, and into the Pacific Ocean by way of the Colorado River. The feds picked a canyon 35 miles east of Las Vegas as the location for the giant dam that would stop up the river and create behind it one of the largest reservoirs in the world.

So while the rest of the country was suffering through the Great Depression, Las Vegans were watching thousands of workmen climb off trains each day to be bused to the tent city erected at the dam site, knowing that come the weekend, these same workers would be right back in town, with full pockets, looking for a good time.

Meanwhile, the political bosses up in Carson City, Nevada's capital, were busy enacting the laws necessary to provide the state with legalized gambling and quickie divorces. When downtown began to fill up with wide-open casinos and celebrity divorcees were covered in the southern California press, Las Vegas had arrived.

The completion of Hoover Dam in 1935 allowed the residents to catch their collective breath until World War II, when thousands of servicemen were deposited at the old Las Vegas Gunnery School, now Nellis Air Force Base. The downtown casinos welcomed the airmen with lively entertainment, full-shot cocktails, and a fair roll of the dice. Having been subjected to shoddier treatment by quick-buck merchants in other parts of the country, the servicemen appreciated the fair shake extended in Las Vegas, where the operators knew that they'd still wind up with their share of the Gunnery School payroll without having to resort to cheating at the tables or watering down the drinks. Judging by the number of former Gunnery trainees who returned to settle in Las Vegas after the war, that philosophy paid off.

Las Vegas' horizons expanded again when hotel tycoon Tommy Hull got a flat tire just south of town during a drive from Los Angeles to Salt Lake City in 1940. While he waited for a tow truck to arrive, Hull counted the out-of-state cars passing by on the old Los Angeles highway (now the Strip) and had a vision of what the patch of desert where he was stuck could become.

Hull acquired the land at the intersection of what is now Las Vegas Boulevard South and Sahara Avenue, and in 1941 opened El Rancho Vegas — at the time the only structure of any kind within a three-mile radius and the last human activity from Las Vegas to Baker, California, 90 miles away.

Hull, who also owned the famed Hollywood Roosevelt Hotel and the El Rancho Sacramento, installed a huge swimming pool right next to the highway, enticing motorists into the resort. The hotel itself was a series of single-story bungalows that surrounded a central building housing the casino, lobby, and restaurants. Everything was swamp-cooled (the air-conditioning of the time).

A year later, Hull's hotel was joined, about two miles south on Highway 91, by the Last Frontier, built by movie-theater magnate R. E. Griffith. Both resorts ran smoothly, but fairly quietly, through World War II, with visitor counts held down by gasoline rationing. The operators of the gambling houses were still happy. They had plenty of business coming in from the Gunnery School, along with busloads of soldiers arriving every weekend from an Army base in Tonopah, about 230 miles northwest.

What would soon become known as "the Strip" got a big boost in 1946, when New York underworld figure Benjamin Siegel opened his Flamingo Hotel. Siegel had grown up as a street punk in New York City, where he was befriended by another budding Jewish hoodlum named Meyer Lansky. As Lansky moved up in the ranks of the underworld, he took his boyhood friend along with him. Lansky eventually became the boss-of-bosses of the Mafia in the

United States, succeeding Charles "Lucky" Luciano, after Luciano was deported by the feds to his native Sicily.

Lansky, who'd served as the key financial expert for the mob for many years, quickly overcame some hard feelings over a Jew being named the top man in the traditionally Italian organization. Lansky moved his headquarters to Miami Beach to be closer to the mob's major gambling action throughout the Caribbean.

In the early 1940s, when Lansky decided that Las Vegas might be ready for development by his organization, he sent Ben Siegel, who'd picked up the nickname "Bugsy" (which he hated), to the desert wasteland to survey the situation. Siegel first muscled into the downtown joints, so he wasn't unfamiliar with the environment when he started scouting property on the old L.A. Highway to achieve a personal dream: of building a palatial resort close to all the glamour in Hollywood. (Siegel's real estate agent knew his way around the desert. He'd been selling porperty to unsuspecting southern Californians who, whether shrewd or stupid, wound up owning some of the most valuable real estate in the world.)

Siegel knew exactly what he wanted for the site of his Flamingo Hotel. First, he'd determined that it shouldn't be within sight of the two existing hotels or downtown. He wanted an exclusive location and settled on acreage more than two miles south of the Last Frontier, around the first bend in the road leading out of Las Vegas.

He also wanted to be on the east side of the two-lane highway. The other hotel owners had built on the west side, making it easier for traffic from Las Vegas to enter their properties. But Siegel wasn't concerned with the local residents; he was after the money crowd from Los Angeles, especially Hollywood. A location on the right side of the road would give the northbound traffic easier access to the sweeping driveway he had in mind for the Flamingo. In later years, it became obvious that he'd been correct in this choice. As additional hotels were planned, they were all located on the east side of the road. The west side was used only when all of the choice spots across the street were taken.

Though he was a little ahead of his time in that regard, Siegel couldn't save the Flamingo — or himself — with location. The New York hood had a million dollars of his own money, plus several million of his partners' money, allocated to build his ultra-luxurious dream resort in the middle of nowhere. That budget was badly bruised when he insisted on using prime copper piping for the plumbing throughout. This was in the months following the end of World War II, when copper was still in the hands of the military, and Siegel had to plunge into the black market where he paid highly inflated prices.

Siegel also traveled to areas of the Middle East, where the climate was similar to the southern Nevada desert, to find exotic trees and plants which, he was assured, would flourish in Las Vegas. Even more money was wasted on Siegel's high-priced romance with mob moll Virginia Hill, whom he lavished with extravagant gifts. And then there was Siegel's "public-relations" work in Hollywood: his socializing with entertainers and movie stars to attract them — and, in turn, all their fans — to his new casino. Pipe, palms, perfume, and parties alone came close to eating up the entire building budget.

By the time the Flamingo was ready to open, Siegel had spent more than $5.5 million. He had to swear on his life that he'd repay his partners all their money, plus huge profits, within a year. However, the grand opening of the Flamingo, on December 26, 1946, was a dismal flop. A torrential rainstorm kept the Las Vegans away. Local dignitaries, unhappy with the brash New Yorker, didn't show up either. And most of the Hollywood stars he'd cultivated seemed to have other things to do that night.

About the only positives to come out of the opening were Siegel's discoveries that live flamingos couldn't stand the desert climate (he lost only two of the regal birds before he canceled his order for 100 more) and that his plan for dressing all of the casino dealers in tuxedos would not be acceptable to either the employees or the relaxed Westerners.

Meanwhile, throughout the long grand opening, Siegel was receiving disturbing phone calls from both Miami and New York. Though he initially did a good job of bluffing his way through, his stories quickly got old. After only a few weeks, with no sign of business improving to the point where the property could hope to pay for itself, the Flamingo closed. Siegel had simply spent too much money.

The casino reopened two months later and seemed to be on the verge of turning a profit, but Siegel's fate had been sealed. Lansky did everything he could to help Bugsy, but even he couldn't save his childhood pal from the wrath of the investors. In May 1947, Siegel took a couple of slugs in the head as he sat reading a newspaper in the Beverly Hills apartment of his girlfriend Virginia Hill. Bugsy's body was still warm when Moe Sedway, Morris Rosen, and Gus Greenbaum walked into the Flamingo and took over.

I showed up a few years later.

The Columnist from New York

I'd been introduced to Las Vegas in 1945 by my parents, who periodically loaded my brothers and me into the car and made the miserable eight-hour drive from Los Angeles, straight across the hot Mojave Desert. My dad would rent an "air conditioner" at a desert service station. This unit, called a hydrofan, hung on the passenger window of the car. It was necessary to add about a gallon of water to it every 10 miles or so. The water would pour over the fan blades and the cooler air was supposed to blow into the car. However, when the tank was full, the hydrofan would douse the passengers with a heavy spray. As soon as the water was used up, it was super hot once again. At 12 years old, I thought this was all pretty funny.

My folks could get a room with two double beds for $6 or $7 a night at El Rancho Vegas. All-you-could-eat "chuckwagon" dinners, the forerunner of the buffet, were a buck. Seeing a top-flight entertainer in a fancy showroom was free. If you wanted to eat during the show, you could pay $2.50 or $3 for a complete steak dinner. Gambling subsidized all costs incurred to attract the players and Las Vegas was the least expensive holiday spot in the land. These trips were fun for us kids, too, because we were able to spend all day in and around the hotel swimming pools, or even occasionally slip a nickel into a slot machine and pull the handle. But none of us even dreamed about Las Vegas as a possible future home. It was hot, desolate, and rather ugly. And we were city folk.

In high school, my ambition was to be a professional basketball player, until an injury spelled the end of my athletic career. I then became interested in journalism, worked my way up to sports editor of the school newspaper, and landed a position in a program for high-school sports writers sponsored by the *Los Angeles Examiner* (a now-defunct Hearst newspaper). The Scholastic Sports Association put a bunch of L.A. high-school kids to work writing, copyediting, laying out, and proofreading a weekly spread on high-school sports in the sports section. Then, when I graduated high school, I was offered a job at the *Examiner* as a copy boy. I also went to East L.A. College. But I couldn't carry the full-time school load and work at the same time, so I gave up school.

In 1953, after three years at the *Examiner* and prior to my 20th birthday, a friend advised me that there was a job opening for a cub reporter at the *Las Vegas Sun*. I'd never even heard of the paper, which was fairly new and reportedly funded by the Printers Union in an effort to cut into the business of the established *Las Vegas Review-Journal*. The idea of two daily papers in a market of 44,000 was ridiculous.

Still, I called the editor. I should have been suspicious when he hired me over the phone. But I found out only after I arrived and reported for work that I'd been hired not just as a starting reporter, but as the *only* full-time reporter on the minuscule staff. My duties were to cover all city and county offices, whatever breaking news stories there might be, along with anything else that had to be done.

Not knowing any better, I jumped into the frying pan feet first. Only two weeks later, I found myself in the fire when Bill Willard, the paper's entertainment columnist, quit. I was informed that I would also be writing the daily entertainment column. It was all pretty heady stuff, especially to a green newsman who wasn't even old enough to be inside the casinos legally.

I expanded the column to cover hotel and casino news and quickly became at least acquainted with most of the gambling and political movers and shakers, as well as with the entertainers who were appearing in Las Vegas.

One day, Walter Winchell, at the time the leading newspaper columnist and radio commentator in the country and a regular visitor to Las Vegas, dropped in at the offices of the *Sun*. His column appeared in our paper, as well as in hundreds of other newspapers all over North America. In those days, when TV was still in its infancy, Winchell held the top-rated radio show, which was broadcast around the country every Sunday night and began with his staccato greeting, "Good evening Mr. and Mrs. North and South America and all the ships at sea..."

Winchell congratulated me on my appointment as entertainment columnist and asked if I was heading out to the Strip. He needed a ride. There were seven hotels along Las Vegas Boulevard in 1953, with the Sahara and Sands hotels having just opened their doors, and the El Rancho Vegas, Last Frontier, Flamingo, Thunderbird, and Desert Inn in full swing. Winchell invited me to "make the rounds" with him and we started at the Sands. This new property had been built under the auspices of the Meyer Lansky interests. Jake Freidman, operator of a successful Texas casino, was brought in to run the Sands.

Winchell was unmistakable to the casino patrons that afternoon. His dark-blue custom-made suit, trademark fedora, and silver hair were known to the masses, who'd seen his picture in newspapers and magazines even before he began appearing on his own television show and then as the narrator on the hit TV series, "The Untouchables." He signed a couple of autographs as we walked. While we were passing the large open cocktail lounge of the new hotel, he slowed and then stopped. He was looking toward the center of the room, where seven or eight men were seated around a table, with another half-dozen seated a discreet distance behind them.

Winchell let out a low whistle. "Your education is about to begin," he told me. He gestured toward the center table and pointed out a man who was looking directly at him. "Okay, that's Hymie Barranga, from Detroit." He then pointed around the table and reeled off the names of some of the most notorious gangland figures in the country. "This has got to be serious—for these guys to get together out here. Vegas is supposed to be clean, and here you've got a Mafia council meeting right in the middle of the newest joint in town."

I admitted that I was bewildered by the whole scene. Winchell patiently explained that council meetings were generally called to determine the future of someone who had been accused of some sort of wrongdoing against the "family." The outer circle of men were the bodyguards who protected the members of the council. I asked Winchell if their being seen together by him would scare them off.

"Never happen," he responded. "Within a day or two, some pretty important fish will be found dead." It was just the next day that the body of a top Miami Beach gang leader was discovered along a country road in Florida.

Winchell introduced me to men I'd heard of and to plenty of others whose names meant nothing to me at the time. Most of the names that I recognized had been introduced to all of America during live telecasts of the organized crime hearings that had recently gripped the nation.

The Senator from Tennessee

Television was just coming of age in the early 1950s when Estes Kefauver, the United States senator from Tennessee, along with his Committee to Investigate Organized Crime, traveled throughout the country and held televised hearings on the activities of the mob. Viewers were treated to a continuous parade of witnesses whom they'd read about in the headlines and seen in the movies over the years. As far as the American public was concerned, the Kefauver hearings were all there was on the tube.

The soft-drawling senator and his cohorts from Congress and the media put the spotlight on jurisdictions around the states where criminal activities were most prevalent. Kefauver's committee identified illegal casinos in New York, Kentucky, Arkansas, Florida, Missouri, Illinois, and California and subpoenaed their suspected owners to testify in front of the cameras. That was when some sharp attorney rediscovered the Fifth Amendment to the Constitution, which states that no man can be forced to testify against himself. The droning phrase, "I refuse to testify on the grounds that my testimony may tend to incriminate me," was popularized during the Kefauver hearings.

The illegal casinos drew heavy attention, thanks to the great photographic opportunities. Pictures of cops using axes on gambling tables and slot machines, and reputed hoods being hustled off to jail in handcuffs made for compelling images on front pages and the six o'clock news.

The message wasn't lost on the owners, who were plenty savvy after years of operating successfully underground. The word was spread: "Close up and clear out." Some had to walk away from multimillion-dollar businesses after Senator Kefauver exposed them and the local authorities could no longer look the other way in return for payoffs. Some headed for the Caribbean; others made a beeline for Nevada. In Las Vegas, the Desert Inn opened in 1950, then the Sands and Sahara in 1952. But in the mid-1950s, the Caribbean gravy train dried up when Fidel Castro and his revolutionary forces liberated Havana and kicked out the casino operators almost all in the same day.

That placed virtually all legal casino gambling available for American consumption in Nevada. The underworld controlled the resort industry and, strangely enough, with the exception of the federal income-tax evasion, operated completely within the law. There were no payoffs to cops or politicians. There was no fear of trouble between competitors after it was agreed that there would be absolutely no violence in Las Vegas. The operators were honorable in their business dealings: Written contracts were almost unheard of, a handshake was enough to finalize any deal, and when a boss told you something, you could take it to the bank. The period from about 1950 until the mid-1970s will go down in history as the "golden years" of Las Vegas.

I don't know whether Kefauver realized just how deeply he hurt the underworld, but evidence of it was all over Las Vegas. Virtually every man in any sort of executive position within a local casino operation had a criminal record. If nothing else, there were at least some gambling offenses, which could never be denied. Those individuals, incidentally, made up the majority of the "underworld" in Las Vegas. And here I was, getting a tour of the landscape, less than two years after Kefauver, by Walter Winchell himself.

I was 19 years old, too young to hang around the casinos where I had to gather most of the information for my column and stories. Yet I found myself chatting, on a daily basis, with the town's top politicians, assorted business leaders, notorious hoodlums, and other colorful characters you find hanging around gambling joints. The Sands had just opened, so I spent a lot of my time there; that's where the news was being made. A pair of underworld bosses, Carl Cohen and Sid Wyman, kept an eye on me and made sure I didn't stray from the straight and narrow.

2

Flamingo Fun

I was moving along just fine, reporting news during the day and gathering information for the column at night. I was single, renting a bedroom in a private home, and grateful that the casinos fed me for free in the showrooms. Otherwise, I never would've had a decent meal, given my magnanimous salary of $65 a week. Finally, I went to the paper's publisher, Hank Greenspun, and asked for a raise. When he turned me down (and insulted my commitment to ethical journalism in the process), I had to quit.

I moved back to L.A. and worked a variety of odd jobs until I landed a position as a reporter with the *Los Angeles Herald-Express*. I also got married to my wife of 45 years, Joyce. My tenure at the *Herald-Express* was a newspaperman's dream. I was a general assignment reporter, which meant that I might call the office with a story on a murder and then be told to head out to the Eagle Rock Garden Club to cover a speech by an expert on the pruning of roses.

There was never a dull moment. Like many reporters, I became typecast, and the casting was certainly to my liking. My assignments leaned toward news and crime articles, as well as features, those wonderful stories about off-beat people doing off-beat things, where the writer's imagination is allowed to soar a little.

This was 1955, a time when newspapers and magazines all over the country were sounding the death knell for Las Vegas. According to the media, the town was overbuilt and overrun with hoodlums, pimps and prostitutes, small-time con artists, and the like. It was a hatchet job, pure and simple, perpetrated by some of the nation's most respected writers and respectable publications.

I offered to go to Las Vegas and get an objective view of what was going on. Since the Fremont's grand opening was being held in a few days and the new hotel had invited our paper to cover the festivities, my editor decided that I could use the plane ticket sent by the Fremont and stay on long enough to gather information about the state of the city. I went on a real tear, talking with resort owners and operators, politicians, bankers, and contractors—anyone and everyone familiar with the town's economic condition. I discovered that virtually none of the people I spoke to had ever been interviewed by anyone from the national press that was spinning all the doomsday tales.

After three or four days, I flew back to L.A. and wrote a five-part series on what was really happening in Las Vegas. I tried to show that there had been a bit of overbuilding by some aggressive outsiders who were intent on cashing in on the huge profits being lapped up by the existing properties. I wrote that the biggest problem in the 1955 bust (as has been proven true in most other busts Las Vegas has weathered over the years) was that the new hotels were being built and operated by people from outside the gambling industry. These people, such as the original owners of the Riviera, weren't able to learn the risky business fast enough to avoid going broke.

Into the Lion's Den

A few years after the series appeared, I informed some people I still knew in Las Vegas that I was ready to return to town and try my hand as a "publicist." This was the term used back then to describe a casino executive who today is known variously as director of marketing, vice president of communications, media relations coordinator, or some other high-falutin' title designed to justify an inflated salary. The publicist in the old days was personally responsible for anything and everything involved with the name and reputation of the property he represented. These were the men who spent their bosses' money to transform Las Vegas from a railroad town of 44,000 into the most attractive resort destination in the entire world with a population exceeding one million.

Among Las Vegas' early publicists was a phalanx of PR pros that has never been duplicated—men like Al Freeman, Harvey Diederich, Herb McDonald, Eugene Murphy, Hal Braudis, Larry Sloan, Hank Kovell, Lee Fisher, and Abe Schiller. These were the true movers and shakers who told the Las Vegas story to the entire world in a manner that had men and women salivating to visit this Shangri-la. On their own, collectively, and in conjunction with the Las Vegas News Bureau, they papered the globe with "cheesecake," photos of bathing beauties doing most anything photogenic. Pictures of showgirls and dancers graced front, middle, and back pages of newspapers and magazines from Alaska to Zanzibar.

The global press found itself under a constant deluge of news releases promoting all facets of the Las Vegas experience. In addition to reams of copy publicizing the fabulous around-the-clock entertainment in virtually every resort, there were stories on expansions, on the volume of food consumed in a single hotel in a single day, and on celebrities visiting or getting married, as well as a variety of puffery on every other aspect of Las Vegas life.

The publicists also worked to keep a clean face on Las Vegas. They launched a campaign promoting the number of houses of worship in the city, which, they claimed, was among the highest per capita in the nation.

When national columnist and humorist Damon Runyon died of cancer, Walter Winchell came to Las Vegas and met with publicist Eugene Murphy at the Desert Inn. The famed resort had just made a deal with the Professional Golf Association to stage a tournament of champions on the golf course behind the hotel. Winchell was looking for a way to announce the formation of — and start collecting donations for — the Damon Runyon Cancer Fund.

Murphy gained approval from the owners of the DI to turn over a percentage of the admission fees and money raised at the opening banquet. Then Wilbur Clark, the dashing operator of the Desert Inn, announced that the hotel would match all money donated to the fund by the golf tournament.

Remember, these were the years that Las Vegas faced heavy opposition from millions of Americans who listened to lengthy sermons against everything the town stood for. (Many Bible Belt states remained lined up against the sinners of southern Nevada for decades, until gambling was legalized in their own domains and the churches found themselves the recipients of sizable donations from casino operators.) Used to fighting that kind of uphill battle, the early press agents and publicity directors were among the most inventive promotors the world has ever seen.

There are still a few original thinkers on the scene to-day who would probably have fit in with that unique group of 40 years ago. However, publicly traded corporations frown on news being handled in a whimsical or inventive way, afraid that it might affect the price of company stock.

Thank goodness that sort of thinking wasn't prevalent when Steve Wynn donned a sourdough miner's costume and did TV commercials for the Golden Nugget, playing the part of Ebenezer Wynn. It was the same kind of show-manship that enabled Wynn to introduce Las Vegas to Wall Street. If he harmed the dignity of the city and its legalized gambling, it certainly hasn't become evident yet.

Anyway, I liked the magic I saw these brilliant artists performing and wanted the opportunity to join them. I knew a group of people who were in the process of purchasing a hotel and I made it clear that I wanted to be their publicist.

A few weeks later, I saw an ad in the L.A. Times classi-fied section seeking a publicist "for a major Las Vegas ho-tel." My first thought was that my people had made their deal and bought the hotel, but that someone below the owners' level had placed the ad. I sent a resume, in case I was right; I kept it sketchy, in case I was wrong. I didn't want to appear desperate for the position—I wasn't really looking for another job, unless it was exactly what I wanted.

About three weeks after I mailed the resume, I had one of the toughest days of my entire newspaper career. I ar-rived for work at eight in the morning as usual. Around noon, a brush fire was reported in the Hollywood Hills. Because it was in a heavily populated area, loaded with mansions and estates, the majority of the staff was sent to cover it. The fire burned the rest of the day and through the long night and we all stayed with it, reporting on the scores of burned homes and injured firemen. In addition, many priceless manuscripts were destroyed when the fire swept through the home of Aldous Huxley. It was a tough night.

I finally dragged myself home at about nine in the morning and was just getting ready for bed when the phone rang. A voice at the other end of the line boomed, "This is Morris Lansburgh."

The name didn't register.

"I'm owner and president of the Flamingo Hotel in Las Vegas."

Now I recalled that I'd heard a Miami Beach hotel tycoon was buying the Flamingo. But I couldn't guess why he was calling me—other than to keep me from getting to sleep. I mumbled something into the phone.

He said impatiently, "You answered our ad for a publicist."

I still had no idea what he was talking about, so the owner of the Flamingo had to describe the ad I'd seen in the *L.A. Times* before I finally remembered.

"Oh, was that *your* ad?" I inquired. "I thought it was placed by someone else."

He had to wonder what kind of a nut I was. But he demanded that I immediately fly to Las Vegas so he could interview me. I explained that I was just preparing for sleep after working all night, which made him noticeably upset. But we finally agreed that I would take a short nap, then fly up and meet him at three that afternoon.

Our initial meeting was a fiasco. I walked into the office of Morris Lansburgh, who was joined by Jerry Gordon, vice president and general manager of the hotel. I sat down and they started firing questions at me. I wasn't ready for any of it. I was too tired to think straight and I still had little clue as to who this undistinguished-looking man with the booming voice might be.

That was the first of many times at the Flamingo that I felt I had no choice but to grab center stage and run the show my way—for a while, anyway. "Excuse me, Mr. Lansburgh," I said. "You seem to know a lot about me, but I must admit I don't know anything about you. Matter of fact, I don't even know how you spell your last name."

He chuckled and spelled his name, then told me some of his own story. He was president of eight major resort hotels in flourishing Miami Beach and had come to Las Vegas a few months earlier to operate the Flamingo for a group of investors. He told me how he'd begun his career by taking over a bankrupt hotel on Collins Avenue in Miami Beach. A banker, who'd been captivated by the brash young man, provided him with enough money to operate the hotel for a few months, at least through the winter season.

Lansburgh moved in and went to work. First, he became friendly with some politicians and prevailed upon them to place a pedestrian traffic signal in front of his hotel. That way, people could push the button and stop traffic while they crossed the busy boulevard. He then printed up some colorful fliers that extolled the virtues of his hotel. Lansburgh's son Leonard and his daughter Ellen were stationed on either side of the street. His son Mickey was still too young to be out in traffic, so he stood by the signal and waited until a suitable number of cars approached, at which time he'd push the button, turning the light to red and giving Leonard and Ellen enough time to drop a circular into the front seat of every car.

As Lansburgh's hotel empire grew, he continued to come up with new promotional ploys to attract more guests. He was the man who instituted travel packages, so popular in today's market. He also introduced "Dine Around," which allowed guests staying in one of his hotels to dine at any of his properties as part of an American Plan package. And he started the "Cavalcade of Stars," where he booked the top names in entertainment into the huge showroom at his Deauville Hotel and made the shows available to guests in all of his properties as part of their prepaid packages. ·

In Las Vegas, he doubled the size of the Flamingo from 400 to 800 rooms. He built the first hotel convention center. In 1961, he established the famed Candlelight Room, the first gourmet restaurant at any Vegas property. He originated gamblers' junkets and introduced package travel to southern Nevada.

Trying to keep up with the man at that initial meeting while I was so tired was unfair to both of us. I finally got him to agree to postpone it until the next morning. In the meantime, I found out a few more things about Morris Lansburgh. My Las Vegas sources informed me that he had one of the greatest promotional minds in the resort industry. In addition to his Dine Around and Cavalcade of Stars programs, he introduced the "Modified American Plan," which provided his guests with breakfast and dinner, but dropped lunch, which is rarely eaten by travelers.

The following morning, Lansburgh and I were at it again, and we had a whale of a knock-down drag-out fight. It seemed that although we were headed toward the same destination, we were taking completely different roads. I didn't like the man, and it was quite obvious that he didn't much care for me. I think Jerry Gordon had the best time. He really got a kick out of us discussing, debating, and finally arguing about all sorts of things. Still, by late that afternoon, our personal war had settled into a truce. Lansburgh said he would call me, and I made it clear I was interested in working with him, even though I could see it would be a challenge every day.

A week later, Lansburgh called and offered me the job. But he made it clear that it would be a 30-day trial period, and if things didn't work out, we would part company. I couldn't believe it: He was offering me a post that neither of us expected to last more than a month. I had tenure at the *Herald-Express*. I had a wife and two babies. I was supposed to give up my job and move my family with only a 30-day guarantee? Still, I was determined to make this man eat his words, and I brashly accepted the job offer.

When I returned to Los Angeles and broke the news to Joyce, she expressed confidence in me, even after I told her that in the short time Lansburgh had been in Las Vegas, he'd already gone through three or four publicists. Her faith reinforced what I already knew: She was as nutty as I was!

I then went to see Captain James Hamilton, head of the L.A. Police Department's Intelligence Division, the first such unit ever set up, later copied by police departments around the world. I opposed Hamilton and his collection of "spies," and I disapproved of William Parker, the chief of police who determined that he needed to know everything about anyone who might be (or might become) one of his enemies, including members of organized crime, politicians, business leaders, attorneys, and newspaper reporters. I opposed Hamilton, but I still had a cordial working relationship with him, and thus was able to find out what I was getting myself into at the Flamingo.

I knew the Flamingo wasn't being run by a group of choir boys, but I wanted to know beforehand if there was anyone associated with the property I should steadfastly avoid. The notorious Meyer Lansky was at the top of the list, as I'd anticipated. But I knew that from the time of the Kefauver organized-crime hearings, Lansky had never again set foot in Las Vegas. Even his brother Jake had cut way back on his forays to the desert.

As for the other partners, some names were known to me and others were not. However, their supposed percentage points of ownership in the Flamingo were small enough to ensure that they actually had no say in the operation.

Then I came across a card on "Nigger" Sam Cohen, complete with a photograph providing ample evidence for the nickname. The man had Caucasian features, but his skin was swarthy to the point that he might easily be mistaken for a black man. The card attributed a criminal record to Sam Cohen that wouldn't stop. He was said to be a close associate of most of the major crime lords throughout the country and was shown to be the owner of more than 30 percent of the Flamingo. Clearly, this was a man to avoid.

After I began working at the Flamingo, Sam Cohen happened to be at the hotel for one of his usual visits and we were introduced. I looked at the man and thought back to the intelligence-file picture and description of him. This was not the same man. I soon learned that our Sam Cohen owned numerous apartment buildings in New York City, which brought him a monthly fortune. He was a business associate of Meyer Lansky, but had no criminal record whatsoever. The LAPD files were totally wrong. This bore out a long-held contention of mine that the elite L.A. Intelligence Unit had some major faults in the ways it collected and corroborated information, and in the conclusions it drew.

Shortly after meeting Cohen, I ran into Jim Hamilton, who was in Las Vegas to make a speech at a police intelligence convention. I informed him of the glaring error in his investigative files and he tried to recruit me to provide him with correct information on Cohen and a number of other people whose files he felt could be fattened.

I respectfully (or maybe not so respectfully) declined.

However, I filed this incident for future reference and realized that the old adage still rang true: "Believe nothing of what you hear and only half of what you see."

A Babe in the Woods

On my first day at the Flamingo, I reported for work wearing a sports shirt, slacks, and a sweater. Lansburgh immediately called me into his office. He explained that his executives wore suits and ties at all times. I already knew that most of the Flamingo executives had come West from Miami Beach, where the three-piece suit was considered *de rigueur*. Many of the guests stayed at the big resort hotels while conducting business in the city, and those who were there for vacation all tried to impress one another. But Las Vegas, even then, had more of a "come-as-you-are" attitude, where guests were attired as they pleased.

I explained my view that our customers would feel more relaxed if they were greeted by hotel executives who were attired much the same as they were. Being familiar with Las Vegas, I also knew that what impressed visitors the most was the totally relaxed and friendly atmosphere. Everyone working at the resort hotels understood that the guests came to Las Vegas to escape their lives for a while — to let their hair down. Of course, we all had to put a lot of work into conveying that impression of a relaxed and casual atmosphere!

Lansburgh, for example, spent much of his time circulating through the hotel and casino and greeting guests, so he understood my point and agreed to allow me to dress in this manner, again on a trial basis. But I agreed that when I was in the hotel after dark, it was suit-and-tie time. It became a gag around the hotel. When employees saw me wearing a jacket and tie during the day, they assumed I was going either to a funeral or out of town. Then they started saying the same thing about Lansburgh, once he followed my lead.

Soon, many of the Flamingo executives were wearing

leisure clothes. The casino bosses, however, never adopted the casual look. At that time, every casino boss in town wore the same basic uniform, with few variations on the theme: black silk suits, white-on-white silk shirts, either solid black or solid white neckties, spit-polished shoes, huge cuff links, and a bulge in an area around one of the inner breast pockets of the suit. In the eyes of the public, that bulge could be only one thing: a gun.

I recall a trip I made to Phoenix, where I attended a cocktail party for travel agents. The host introduced me around as a representative of the Flamingo Hotel in Las Vegas. For the rest of the evening, I was made to feel rather uncomfortable by the other guests, who seemed to be watching my every move. As the evening progressed, one young woman, apparently having had more than her share of cocktails, tried to walk purposefully toward me (it was more like a stagger). With her face nearly touching my chest, she looked up and declared, "You don't scare me, buster."

To see her better, I reached into my inner breast pocket to remove my eyeglasses. I heard gasps from around the room and noticed all the frightened expressions. So I simply smoothed my jacket and excused myself. I have no doubt that the guests at that party told their friends that they'd met a real live Las Vegas hoodlum.

Anyway, Lansburgh and I made it through that first month, then continued on a month-to-month basis. Our dislike for each other continued and, alternately, he wanted to fire me and I wanted to quit. Slowly, however, the polar ice cap between us began to melt. One time, Lansburgh and I had been sniping at one another most of the morning. He was sitting in his office, which was down the hallway from mine. Phones or intercoms weren't used. If he wanted someone, he yelled for him. On this particular day, he yelled for me in such a way that it raised the hair on the back of my neck. I jumped out of my chair and stormed down the hall. Lansburgh took one look at my face, jumped up, and stood behind his desk chair, as if seeking protection.

His terrified response was too much. I advanced to his desk, put my hands down flat on the desktop, and laughed openly. Things started improving after that.

However, I must admit that Morris Lansburgh went to great lengths to be nice to his guests. And those guests never forgot him. Anytime he came out of his office, he'd greet guests. He would walk into the coffee shop and stroll through the room speaking with people seated at every table. It got to the point where comedian Jack Carter, who performed at the Flamingo regularly, included the Lansburgh greetings in his act. He would talk about Lansburgh, then walk around the stage, bowing and extending his hand, and saying, "Good evening, telephone." "How are you, drapes?" "Are you enjoying yourselves, forks and spoons?" It was one of Carter's best-received bits, since most of the audience had experienced the real thing. It was also Carter who hung Lansburgh with the nickname "Mr. Bow," because of the way he used to bend at the waist when greeting guests.

Another effective management policy Lansburgh enforced was that all his executives had to stay out of the "Ivory Tower" for at least two hours a day and spend that time talking to guests, helping to solve problems and, generally, being good-will ambassadors. In that way, very few of our guests were overlooked. It was a lot of work for all of us, but the guests certainly appreciated it. What's more, we found that the Lansburgh style of operation gave every one of us a thorough knowledge of what was going on in every other department on the property. All the executives got along and never felt they had to protect themselves from one another.

Another mark in Lansburgh's favor was that he gave his entire executive staff fairly free rein. When an idea was brought to him, he usually said, "If you like it, run with it." That was how the International Press Christmas Party came to be.

Shortly after joining the Flamingo staff, I attended a meeting of the Las Vegas public-relations committee, comprised of all the PR people in town. The committee's official duty was to oversee the operations of the all-important Las Vegas News Bureau.

At this meeting, Gene Murphy, Herb McDonald, and Al Freeman, a trio of promotional giants, had apparently decided it was time to "welcome" me to the group. Murphy got it rolling, addressing the "problem of all those damned freeloading newspapermen looking to bring their whole families up here during the busy summer season."

McDonald then chimed in, "Freeloading, of course."

Less than a month earlier, I'd been one of "them," and I chafed at the remarks about newspapermen.

Freeman, who probably had the best worldwide press contacts of anyone at the meeting, had to get his two nasty cents in, naming my journalist fraternity the "freeloading Fourth Estate."

Oh, did they have me hooked!

As soon as there was a slight pause in the attack, I jumped to my feet to defend all those members of the working press who were being so vilified.

"Look," I half yelled, "any newsman you can buy for the price of a meal or a complimentary room isn't worth buying. The majority of reporters and editors up and down the line are dedicated to reporting the news, not to seeing how much they can freeload."

Everyone was attentive. I had them. So like the greenhorn I was, I pressed my luck. I went on the bluff: "I'm working on a promotion right now that will bring hundreds of newsmen to the Flamingo as paying guests. And these will include some of those newspeople that every one of us would be more than happy to comp if they would just stay in our hotels."

There was some laughter, and then the meeting ended. On my drive back to the Flamingo, I realized that I'd allowed three expert needlers to get to me in a big way. Now, somehow, I had to come up with a promotion that would do what I'd just promised.

It took me about a week to formulate the plans for the first annual International Press Christmas Party.

First, I picked the second week of December — then, as now, the slowest time of the year in Las Vegas. Then I decided we would stage an event that would attract anyone who worked in the editorial end of a newspaper office. This would encompass publishers all the way down to copy boys. All members of the press would be treated equally during this one event of the year.

Lansburgh nodded (slightly) when I told him of my plans for getting outside interests to sponsor some of the parties and meals. I produced a brochure and mailed it to every daily newspaper in the country, as well as to a few foreign newspapers, inviting their staffs to attend the event. I reduced our normal room rates to half, a reasonable discount for the slow season.

And then I waited.

I had no idea what kind of response to expect and no idea about potential sponsors or entertainment. All the while I was getting daily phone calls from my tormentors, asking when I would show them the big promotion that would prove newsmen weren't freeloaders.

A week after mailing the brochures, I received a phone call from Whit Henry of the San Francisco Press and Union

League Club asking for more information. He told me a group of newsmen was thinking of chartering an airplane and coming to the party. I promised to fly to San Francisco early the next week for further discussion.

As I hung up, my secretary told me that Bernie Sedley, editor of the daily paper in Tucson, was on the phone. Bernie wanted to talk about the party, too; the small town (at that time) of Tucson had already fielded a busload to attend. The response was overwhelming from all over the country. There were even a couple of good-sized groups from Canada.

I held to my commitment that all newspeople would be treated equally. A powerful newspaper columnist from Los Angeles, who was also a long-time friend, called to tell me that he and his significant other (also a major columnist) wanted to come to the party. This particular columnist was the epitome of a freeloading newspaperman. He wouldn't pay for anything and could have stayed at the Flamingo free anytime he wanted — except to attend this party.

When I filled him in on the situation, he told me he would call me back. I didn't get another call. But in the mail a couple of days later, there was his registration application, along with a check — drawn on the account of a famous movie studio.

Sponsors, meanwhile, came running. That first year they included British Overseas Airways, Schlitz Beer, Frito-Lay and Pepsi-Cola (at that time separate companies), and Petrocelli Clothes.

Now that the Press Christmas Party was established (it would continue for all the years I remained at the Flamingo), it was time to go for more. I thought about filling the hotel in January, which was about as slow as December, and came up with the Travel Agents Winter Showcase. In this promotion we gave away all our rooms to the men and women we were hoping would help keep them filled the rest of the year. It worked. Within six months following the first event, the Flamingo Hotel was booking more travel agency business than all the other Las Vegas resorts combined.

Finally, about a year after I'd started working at the Flamingo, Lansburgh called me into his office one morning and closed the door—a rarity. Jerry Gordon, the general manager, was also there, looking grim. I immediately began thinking about where I might seek employment that afternoon.

Lansburgh sat down. "Dick," he began, seriously. "I don't like you. I don't like the way you do your job. Everything you do is wrong in my book. I'd love to get rid of you. But, goddamn it, you get results. I don't know how or why. But the things you do always seem to work." He shook his head and gave me a wry smile. "So from now on, you make your own decisions and do things your way. I've already told this to Jerry and I'm repeating it to you in front of him. Jerry will stay out of your way. If you want some help from any of us, fine. Otherwise, you're on your own."

I'd finally been accepted. And that was how it remained for another six years.

3

Subdividing the Valley

Anyone who's visited Las Vegas any time within the past 30 years or so knows the dazzling Strip as a seething surging flood of humanity. Throngs crowd sidewalks that are wider than most country roads. The roadway itself is, most of the time, a four-mile-long parking lot, with traffic jammed into three lanes on each side, all six lanes going nowhere. A couple dozen traffic signals line the Strip, controlled by the central traffic computer.

Parking for the thousands of cars attempting to reach destinations along the Strip is provided by sprawling lots and high-rise structures that dwarf many of the largest hotels built back when I came to town. The valet parking areas are so vast that it can take as long as a half-hour for an attendant to deliver your car, at which time you're expected to tip him a recommended $2 for bringing it. Of course, if you want your trusty steed parked nearer the entrance, figure on handing the attendant at least five bucks when you give him your car and the same when he gives it back.

The traffic and parking situations today are particularly

perturbing to those of us who recall when it was not only legal, but actually expected, for you to park your car either right in front of a hotel or at the curb of the Strip itself, which was known then as South Fifth Street. Trying either these days will get your vehicle towed to the police impound yard — and get you towed to a psychiatric ward.

The Strip's First Traffic Light

I remember the long hard fight that Jack Cortez, publisher of Las Vegas' first weekly entertainment magazine, *Fabulous Las Vegas*, waged to get the first traffic light installed on the Strip. It was around 1960 and Cortez used his magazine, which was placed in every hotel room in town, to climb onto his soap box and demand a traffic signal at the intersection of the Strip and what was then known as Fulcher Road. At the same time, the original Convention Center was under construction at the intersection of Fulcher and Paradise roads, and Cortez thought it was critical to have some traffic safety at that spot as well. He made innumerable appearances before the County Commission to plead his case.

The commissioners finally threw Jack a bone and installed a stop sign at the dark and barren intersection, recently paved, that fronted the Convention Center. Heartened by that success, Cortez redoubled his efforts for traffic control at his pet intersection, which, he rightfully realized, was the virtual center of the Strip with an equal number of major businesses north and south of the corner. He made regular appearances before the County Commissioners, the Planning Board, and any other board that would listen to him. He presented all sorts of elaborate graphs and charts, plus statistics and other numbers (which were never attributed to anyone) enumerating pedestrian and vehicular accident counts and incident reports.

On the opposing side were all the hotel owners and operators along the Strip who didn't want their thoroughfare saddled with electric traffic control. Some owners even suggested they'd fade the expense of hiring a private traffic cop to be stationed at this one intersection whenever needed. The idea drew a bit of favorable attention as something quaint from which the town might derive some favorable publicity. But the whole thing fell apart when the backers presented some drawings to the commissioners showing a stand from which the cop would direct traffic. The big box was covered with casino advertising, which would be sold to pay the traffic director's salary.

Cortez wouldn't give up. He regularly brought along a local businessperson who would ask for a moment of the Commission's time, then pick up the cause where Cortez had last left off, as if Jack had put the words in the parrot's mouth.

At one County Commission meeting, a little old lady, a typical sweet small-town grandma, supposedly from Arizona, asked if she might say a few words that she felt were important for the commissioners to hear. She was allotted three minutes. The woman launched into a tirade about how close she'd come to being hit by a car that was speeding down the Strip at 70 miles per hour as she and her poor old husband tried to cross in front of the Stardust Hotel. She harangued the commissioners about a traffic light at that intersection for a full 15 minutes, with Jack Cortez providing the Greek chorus: "The poor lady!" "Her poor husband!" "You tell 'em!" And "Amen to that!"

It took several years for Cortez to win, but the commissioners finally relented and declared that the traffic signal would be hung and turned on. Fulcher Road would be re-named Convention Center Drive on the same day.

Jack Cortez wasn't about to let the day pass unnoticed and he put together a major celebration. He called on all the entertainers, hotel owners, political leaders, and horsemen's organizations he'd come to know through his *Fabulous Las Vegas* magazine and traffic-light campaign, and Las Vegas wound up with a big parade to celebrate the big day.

Cortez's idea could do nothing but grow. Once the traffic signal was turned on, petitions to place signals at virtually every intersection along the Strip flooded in. With cars and pedestrians stopping for the red light outside the Stardust, all the hotel and business owners all of a sudden wanted the traffic to stop in front of *their* stores, too.

The Dirt Buyers

The traffic signals, the paved intersections, the Convention Center — all indicated a town that was destined to grow. Las Vegas was already in the process of making many millionaires, as we'll see. But some of the largest fortunes were amassed by individuals who never picked up a playing card or a pair of dice. Instead, they invested in desert wasteland and wound up owning incredibly valuable pieces of earth.

One of the first Las Vegas dirt-buying visionaries, a man who tied up (supposedly worthless) real estate to be shared by generations of his family, but never by him, was Artemus Ham. An attorney who settled in Las Vegas not long after the turn of the century, Ham had a respectable practice, considering that the town was still quite wild and knew few lawyers. He also had some foresight. He started buying up vacant lots all over the downtown area, which he believed would one day grow. He didn't need the cash to support his family, so he continued to buy what everyone else considered worthless scrub. The doomsayers were right for many years, even decades.

But, as we all know, Las Vegas grew and grew. This forced businesses to look for expansion land, and invariably every piece of undeveloped commercial land they found turned out to be a piece of Ham property. The Ham family, who'd learned well from their patriarch, made dollars in profit for every penny that foxy old Artemus had paid for all those vacant lots in downtown Las Vegas. Today, Artemus Ham's name graces the concert hall on the campus of the University of Nevada-Las Vegas.

Another early Las Vegan who made many fortunes in the worthless-turned-valuable sands of the Mojave Desert was Ted Griss, a dyed-in-the-wool real estate speculator. Griss never revealed his formula for buying undeveloped land, but it seemed that every time he made a purchase, the value would skyrocket.

Ted Griss was interested in Las Vegas as an up-and-coming travel destination even before Tom Hull bought the barren land at the top of what would become the Strip and began building his El Rancho Vegas. By that time, Griss was the owner of a giant tract of good-for-nothing desert, some 10 miles southeast of El Rancho Vegas, where there weren't any dirt roads and utilities hadn't even been considered. He'd come into a little more than 10,000 acres when the owner used the property to pay off a $4,000 gambling debt. In addition to his real estate prowess, Griss was a skilled gin rummy player; he probably spent as much time playing gin as he did attending to business.

While Tommy Hull was negotiating to purchase all the acreage at the intersection of the Los Angeles Highway and

San Francisco Street (now Sahara Avenue), Griss was hunt-
ing down the owner of the sand adjacent to the site of the
new motor inn Hull was planning to build.

It was reported that Hull paid $100 an acre for the par-
cel on which he established El Rancho Vegas. But Griss
wasn't thinking in such lofty numbers. Even though the
parcel he wanted abutted Hull's property, the land was otherwise valueless, and he set out to convince the owner of
that fact. When the wind blew, dust from the land billowed
across the highway so heavily that cars had to pull over
and wait for visibility to return. In addition, a dry wash cut
directly across the property. Gullywashers turned the entire area into a dangerous flood zone, with an angry river
rushing off the mountains, raging through the desert, then
cutting across the land that Griss coveted. The highway was
automatically closed any time rain fell in the Las Vegas
Valley.

(Flood control was in the distant future. During a steady
rainfall, virtually every dry wash and gulch coming down
from the Spring Mountains would reach flash-flood proportions in moments. Two of the worst spots for flooding
in those early days were the washes between El Rancho
Vegas and the Last Frontier, and the one that dissected the
land where the original tower of Caesars Palace now stands.
Since most of the settled portion of Las Vegas was on a natural incline leading east from the mountains, every street
became a river, but damage was generally light.)

Griss picked a dark and stormy day to visit the owner
of the property, which consisted of thousands of acres running along the highway from the south end of El Rancho
Vegas to what is now Stardust Road. To the west, the property extended clear back to the Union Pacific Railroad right-
of-way. Griss proposed to buy a mile of highway frontage
that was more than a half mile deep. The deal was cut in

the middle of a gin rummy game. Griss told me he paid $1 a front foot for the entire parcel (a front foot is 12 inches wide and runs all the way to the rear of the property), which worked out to a little more than $5,000.

Griss' deal made him the owner of a piece of land that Circus Circus, Slots A Fun, Westward Ho, and the Stardust occupy today, along with the topless bars and porn shops, limo and bus yards, bars, athletic clubs, Paul-Son Gaming Supplies, and miscellaneous stores, shops, and warehouses strung along Industrial Road. It would be impossible to calculate how valuable the plot of land Ted Griss landed in 1940 for $5,000 would be worth today.

Meanwhile, the worthless desert acreage he won in that monster run at gin rummy was also paying off. Griss found some natural warm springs sprinkled around the land and the area quickly became a favorite gathering place for the locals. He named it Warm Springs Ranch, and then ignored it for years. Over the decades, developers bought chunks of the ranch piecemeal, until 25,000 houses filled it.

Watching the Warm Springs village emerge slowly from the ranch always made me smile. I liked to drive to the area with my wife Joyce and our kids, Jeff and Robin, to see how far the development had spread. In the early '70s, when Jeff and Robin were in their mid-teens, I took them out to the oiled extension of Eastern Avenue, just south of Warm Springs Road, to give them driving lessons.

I also smiled as I viewed the development of the parcel of scrub southwest of Griss' Strip acreage, too far away back then to matter to anyone. Our family would head out to that unpopulated patch with our handguns and rifles for target practice. Our favorite spot for shooting back then is today the lobby of the Gold Coast.

When I first went to work for the *Las Vegas Sun* in the early 1950s, the paper's advertising manager was a tall cowboy named Norm White. White dressed strictly western, with custom-made boots and belts and hats — and a twang to match. He sold print ads by day and evangelized at night about the glories of real estate in the Paradise Valley section of the landscape. White lived in a spartan home at the convergence of two dusty trails that later became the intersection of Flamingo and Paradise roads. He sank his commission checks into every bit of acreage he could buy toward the southeast of town.

Since no one else had any interest in the barren area, White was able to make maximum purchases with minimal outlay. At one point he offered to cut me in on some of his land deals. However, my meager salary at the *Sun* precluded any thought of it. The $5 per week that White wanted me to invest would have knocked out my laundry and haircut money. I opted for personal hygiene over investing in a few dozen acres of nowhere. I knew I was right.

Housing developments and commercial frontage started spreading out toward the southeast in the late 1950s. The first choice for home developers was Paradise Valley and they all wound up on Norm White's doorstep. But it seemed White saw more value in his land than they did. So they swung their sights clear around to the other side of the valley. The only major landowner on the western side of the valley was Howard Hughes. In the early 1950s, he'd picked up 25,000 acres from about the middle of the valley up to the scarp of the Spring Mountains in a shrewd land swap with the federal government. Hughes told the feds he was planning to build a huge industrial park on the land, known as Husite in order to relocate his big defense-industry factories from Los Angeles. They fell for it and traded two 25,000-acre parcels, the second abutting the north end of the Nuclear Test Site near Tonopah. The government got an extension of its restricted military zone, while Hughes got what is known today as Summerlin and Sun City.

In addition to Hughes' property, the western edge of town consisted of a collection of small parcels owned by World War II veterans who'd been allowed to buy federal land in Nevada for $5 per acre (the land was granted on a lottery basis). Southern Nevada home developers turned their real estate agents loose, and the agents contacted the veterans who owned the five-acre parcels, offering to buy them for $125 each. Promised a $100 profit on their unseen property, thousands of them sold.

Two men I knew who'd been stationed in Nevada and purchased their allotted five acres came back for a visit and decided to look at their property. We drove out West Charleston Boulevard to the location of their land, at what's now Decatur Boulevard. They had adjacent lots on the only undeveloped corner of that busy intersection, which they were able to sell immediately for a king's ransom.

Still, the demand for Paradise Valley property wouldn't let up. Prospective home buyers who first headed west to check out the new tracts soon noticed that the morning drive into town, where they would surely work, put them right in the glare of the rising sun. On the way home, they'd be driving directly into the setting sun. Also, the west-valley developments had the reputation of being more of the GI cracker-box variety, and the growing cadre of well-paid hotel and casino executives were ready to shell out bigger bucks for the better homes in the better neighborhoods on the east side.

Ultimately, Norm White got his price for all his Paradise Valley property. The last we heard, he'd purchased his own island off the coast of Washington state and was enjoying retirement.

Though he couldn't get me to invest, Norm did manage to convince someone else at the *Sun*, publisher Hank

Greenspun, to buy land farther out on the southeast side selling for half as much as the ocean of greasewood and mesquite that Norm was shoveling into his portfolio. He pointed Greenspun way beyond Paradise Valley, toward an area that the owner was calling, half in sarcasm and half as a sales pitch, Green Valley. This no-man's land wasn't even in Las Vegas; it belonged to the City of Henderson, some 11 miles from downtown. Greenspun wound up as laird of this entire area, which he began developing shortly before his death. His wife Barbara and the rest of the Greenspun clan took over where Hank left off, and Green Valley (which now has some grass) is today the loudest property boom in all of Nevada.

Also caught up in the 1950s' Las Vegas real estate craze were two unlikely candidates. Ed Barrick and Sam Ziegman were a pair of retired Omaha bookmakers who'd first come to Las Vegas in the late '40s as investors in the Flamingo; they later bought into the Fremont as well. Both were in their 80s and in tip-top shape. They passed their time taking long walks to tour potential real estate purchases.

Barrick and Ziegman made no bones about it: They were interested in property that had growth value. It was nothing to hear them discussing a piece of land, trying to determine whether it would be 25 years or 40 years or 50 years before it reached its potential. Half the fun for them was realizing that they wouldn't be around to know the results. But buying real estate for its potential was what kept them young, long after the insurance actuaries said they shouldn't be walking around at all.

I got lucky one day and wound up with the two of them in my car. I was on my way downtown from the Flamingo. They happened to catch me in the lobby and asked if they could hitch a ride. Of course, they were welcome. It was a wonderful opportunity to listen to these two men with their real estate hats on.

It was long before freeways criss-crossed the area, so we drove on surface streets for the four-mile ride. I could hear them in the back seat, pointing out the properties they owned.

Ed would say, "We should have bought the building alongside that one, too. You could combine the two properties and build a big laundry facility right in back of the employee parking lot."

Then Sam would chime in with, "We *did* buy the building alongside that one."

"We did?" from Ed.

"Sure! I think."

We drove on.

"That lot over there, Ed — that one's ready to sell for residential."

"Ya' think so, Sam? I'd like to see residential surrounding it before we let it loose. How long do you think that'll take?"

"I don't know. It's a godforsaken patch of desert. I'd guess twenty years," Sam said.

"That short? I was thinking more like forty. The future is looking mighty bright for right around the turn of the century."

Just then Barrick asked me to pull the car alongside a huge vacant lot. Before the wheels stopped, Ed was selling his lifelong friend and partner on the virtues of this particular tract of commercial real estate.

"Now this one has potential. Here's your dirt for twenty years from now. I happen to know homebuilders are already quietly starting to buy up land around it. Couple decades, this area should really catch fire."

I laughed to myself. Yeah, about the time each of the men were celebrating his 110th birthday, this lot would be ripe for selling. (Both lived to be in their 90s.)

In his declining years, Ed Barrick still enjoyed a nip or two before heading home for the evening. Flamingo Casino Manager Chester Simms kept an eye on Barrick and if he ever appeared to have had one too many, Simms would have someone drive Barrick home.

One night Barrick decided he didn't want a nursemaid, so he sneaked out of the Flamingo and drove himself home. He made it safely to his driveway. But when he got out of the car, a young tough was waiting to mug him. Standing about five-foot-four and weighing perhaps 140 pounds dripping wet, Ed Barrick had always been, and still was, a fighter. Spotting his assailant half a foot, 50 or 60 pounds, and the same number of years, Barrick threw himself into the robber, who stood pointing a gun at him.

The thief pistol-whipped Barrick, cutting his face and head, but it was the mugger who ran from the scene, nursing his own injuries.

The solid investments Ed Barrick and Sam Ziegman made continue to pay off handsomely for the citizens of Las Vegas. Ed Barrick's widow, Marge, is one of the largest individual donors to the University of Nevada-Las Vegas. She has endowed buildings, entire schools, and the natural history museum.

4

Everyone's a Comedian

The Flamingo, of course, was the house that Benjamin Siegel built, and even in the early 1960s, nearly 20 years after his untimely demise, numerous guests had Bugsy on the brain. Whenever we housed anyone in the penthouse apartment in the Oregon Building that Siegel had built for himself, someone on the staff would make certain to tell the guest this was the penthouse where Bugsy and Virginia Hill had played house — our very finest accommodation.

During the brief period Siegel and Virginia Hill shared the penthouse, an assistant manager was always assigned to man a desolate desk on the mezzanine of the four-story building. In addition to the desk, he had a chair and a telephone. That was all. His total duties consisted of keeping his ears open for any raised voices coming from the penthouse. Siegel and Hill reportedly had some serious battles that would have rivaled some of today's championship boxing matches. When one of the brouhahas began getting loud, the assistant manager telephoned the manager at the front desk. No more rooms would be rented in the building until peace again reigned.

Shortly after I joined the Flamingo staff, a guest came to my office to tell me about something he was certain had been overlooked: a bullet hole in the wall behind one of the living-room sofas. I apologized gravely and assured him I would notify the proper parties. Since there had never been any reports or even rumors of shots being fired in the penthouse, we just added it to the list of tall tales gleaned from occupants of the apartment.

One woman claimed to find a pair of Virginia Hill's underpants "clear at the back of a dresser drawer" — a mere 20 years and countless guests who'd all somehow overlooked it.

Bugsy's Safe

After Hilton Hotels bought the Flamingo in 1971, Jim Seagrave, the public relations director, found "Bugsy's" safe — under his desk. I'd found the same safe when workmen came to replace the carpet in that office while I occupied it. I asked about the safe and was told by the hotel's chief engineer, Don Garvan, that it was one of several floor safes installed when the hotel was built. The door on this particular safe was kept unlocked so the curious — or nosy — could see for themselves that it was empty.

At some point after my discovery of the unlocked and empty safe, someone apparently relocked it. It stayed that way until Seagrave spotted it during another change of carpeting. But Seagrave turned the safe into a media event. He put out a press release about "Bugsy Siegel's private vault," and soon half of Las Vegas was talking about what might be in the safe. Speculation on the contents included millions of dollars in cash, stolen jewels, even body parts. It was a big story.

Long afterward, in 1972, Seagrave finally got to a national television program interested in the story. The TV crew planned to open the safe before an international audience. Some of my compatriots and I were among those contributing to the mass hysteria. We knew the safe was empty, but when the story first broke, we all agreed we would deny ever knowing of its presence, even though we'd all stepped on it who knows how many times.

The big day arrived. A top safecracker and some beautiful girls appeared before the cameras for the "grand opening." I watched it on TV at home. They did a marvelous job building the mystery for about 57 minutes of the hour-long show. Finally, the safecracker succeeded in unlocking the door. The TV personality pulled back the cover, reached his hand down into the dark void, and retrieved a single paper clip — the entire contents of the safe.

If that safe still sits in the floor of the publicity office of the Flamingo, someone should be rediscovering it again fairly soon. After all, that carpeting is about due to be replaced.

Redecorating an Office

As I mentioned earlier, the executives at the Flamingo got along famously — until an opportunity to play a practical joke arose. One of the best I ever experienced came on the day that Flamingo General Manager, Jerry Gordon, returned from the first vacation he had taken in more than 10 years. Before he left, we'd all kidded him about his lack of time off and joked that he was afraid to go, in fear that he might be replaced.

A new entertainment director had been hired at the hotel a couple of weeks before Jerry left on vacation, and the two hadn't hit it off too well on first impressions. We decided to use this strained undercurrent for our practical joke. We had a new nameplate made, bearing the name of the entertainment director, and placed it on Jerry's office door. Inside the office, we put another new nameplate on the desk and stripped the office of Jerry's papers and mementos. Then we had the locksmith rekey the door.

I was sitting in my office on the day Jerry returned. He paused at my door and asked how things were. I was primed. "Oh, everything's about as usual, Jer. You know Lansburgh. Always with his changes. I personally think he went too far this time, but we'll have to wait and see."

Jerry walked to his own office. I heard him try to work his key in the lock. I assumed that was when he saw the changed nameplate on the door, because I heard a slight nervous chuckle. Then he walked back past my office. A couple of minutes later he was back, accompanied by one of the maintenance engineers, who knew nothing of the joke. The engineer used his master key to unlock the door and then left. Jerry entered and found everything changed. He picked up the telephone and asked the operator to page Morris Lansburgh, who was also in on the plot.

Lansburgh told him how busy he was and that he couldn't talk right then. He invited Gordon to meet him for breakfast in the coffee shop the next morning. Now, Jerry Gordon was meticulous about himself, his attire, and even his mannerisms. But when he showed up to meet Lansburgh the next morning, he looked totally disheveled, like a man who'd slept in his clothes, if he'd slept at all.

Once he walked into the coffee shop and found virtually every executive of the hotel sitting and waiting for him, he knew he'd been had. Jerry, who went on to become executive host and vice-president for Caesars Palace and the Desert Inn, never totally forgave any of us.

Meat Well Done

Then there was the Candlelight Room. Morris Lansburgh, who introduced many new elements to the Las Vegas scene, decided at the behest of the casino manager, Chester Simms, to build the first fine-dining restaurant in a casino-resort. Up until then, every hotel had a coffee shop and a dinner show, but there was little call for a gourmet room. The majority of visitors were in Las Vegas to gamble, and take in the fabulous entertainment and enjoy a greatly underpriced dinner in the showroom at the same time.

Simms wanted this special restaurant for his high rollers. He described what he envisioned to his purchasing agent, Steve Delmont. Delmont ran with the idea and developed an almost unbelievable adventure in dining. The Candlelight Room opened in 1961. It was situated away from the noise of the casino, built to seat no more than 60 guests. There was a five-stool mahogany bar, where customers could wait for their tables.

All the furnishings were designed exclusively for the room. Every chair was made of fine leather. The flatware, china, and crystal were special-ordered. Delmont went to the firm that supplied the hotel's meat and instructed it to build a custom locker for Candlelight Room beef. He then visited the packing house, where he hand-picked steaks and roasts and had them transferred to the special locker for longer aging. No meat was ever served at the Candlelight without Delmont's personal approval. And he hired Chef Albert, one of the country's finest gourmet chefs, to turn out steaks, chops, and seafood that Las Vegas diners had never before experienced. He also allowed Albert to make some of his favorite dishes to serve to the hotel bosses.

The blue-ribbon steaks were lopped off the sirloin by Albert. He cut the meat while doing various other chores and I made the mistake one day of asking how he knew the steaks each weighed the 22 ounces that we advertised. He became upset (a usual thing) and challenged me to weigh them. I weighed six separate steaks and every one was within a half-ounce of the advertised cut.

Delmont liked to go on wild shopping sprees, locating items that were virtually unknown in Las Vegas back then, such as confetti sugar, pickled brussel sprouts for martinis, huge strawberries in the middle of winter, even miniature turkeys for smaller parties on Thanksgiving.

What was probably Las Vegas' greatest loss leader up to that time materialized when Delmont decided to be the first to bring in live Maine lobsters on a daily basis. Before this, no one had even tried to transport the delicate shellfish fresh to the desert.

Delmont would accept only lobsters weighing a minimum of two-and-a half pounds. They were sent in each afternoon from Boston on the first direct jet flight to Las Vegas. A steward would meet the plane each day, open the cartons containing the lobsters in native seaweed, and poke at them with a wooden pole. If the lobsters were lively enough to attack the stick, they were acceptable. However, if they appeared at all sluggish, the order would be refused. Chef Albert said only lively lobsters had the delicate taste that he insisted on.

The Candlelight Room disappeared during the Flamingo's change in ownership in the late '60s. However, when Michael Gaughan built the Barbary Coast right next door to the Flamingo in 1979, one of the first executives he hired was Steve Delmont. Gaughan instructed Delmont to duplicate the old Candlelight Room. Today, that restaurant is known as Michael's, one of the top gourmet rooms in the country.

One Candlelight Room regular was comedian Myron Cohen. Cohen had been a textile salesman for many years before he decided to take the patter he'd been using on his customers and develop it into a nightclub act. He was a man of average height, no hair, and absolutely perfect speech, and he could pass just as easily as a business tycoon from Wall Street as he could an immigrant just off the boat from Europe. The Yiddish accent he used for monologues was hilarious in itself.

Cohen was a favorite of Las Vegas high rollers. Anytime he appeared in the Flamingo showroom, the casino would roar with heavy action. After his shows, he could often be found in the hotel coffee shop or at one of the casino bars, treating his fans to more of his extensive repertoire of stories.

The one about the three Texans who walked into a delicatessen in New York City always hit the mark. These Texans tell the waiter they've heard the deli is famous for its bagels and lox, which they order. In a few minutes, the waiter brings their food. The Texans admire the attractive plates full of food, until finally one of them asks, "Which is the bagel and which is the lox?"

The fans loved Cohen; so did Flamingo Casino Manager, Chester Simms. When Cohen was around, the casino minted money. And, of course, Simms himself enjoyed being regaled by Cohen's endless supply of stories. One of Cohen's happiest days was when Simms handed him a gift box. Cohen opened it and found it filled with business cards identifying him as an "Honorary Pit Boss" at the Flamingo Hotel. Nothing could have thrilled him more. He passed out those business cards everywhere he traveled.

The funniest Myron Cohen story of all involved the Candlelight Room, to which he and his wife Miriam adjourned between shows. Cohen was a George (big tipper), and the staff adored his humor and the large tokes he always left them. But the chef, the temperamental Albert, was no fan of Myron's. Cohen ordered his meat very well done, which was something akin to shoe leather in Albert's eyes. He hated to prepare meat for Cohen.

That never stopped the comedian. One night he and Miriam occupied their usual table and Myron decided he would have lamb chops. As was his custom, he ordered them "very well done." The captain dutifully placed the order in the kitchen, then ran out before Albert could commit mayhem upon him.

After the Cohens ate their appetizers and salads, the captain wheeled up a serving cart. With the usual flourish, he served Mrs. Cohen's meal. Then, with even greater pomp, he placed a platter in front of Myron and slowly removed the polished silver dome, revealing a plate filled with ashes and a couple of pantaloons, which at that time were always served on lamb chops in fine restaurants.

Cohen didn't miss a beat. He picked up his fork and began poking around in the ashes. "I'm sorry, Captain, but you brought me the wrong order."

"No, no, Mr. Cohen," the captain responded, somehow managing to keep a straight face. "Those are the lamb chops very well done."

"I'm truly sorry, Captain," Cohen continued, poking at the ashes. "These are pork chops."

It's Post Time

Another comedian about town was Joe E. Lewis. Along with his downtrodden piano accompanist, Austin Mack, Lewis entertained more Las Vegans and visitors over his years of performing at El Rancho Vegas and the Flamingo than just about any other entertainer. And that includes Frank Sinatra, Dean Martin, and all the other megastars who have appeared here.

Joe E. Lewis was born to be two things: a great nightclub entertainer and an awful horse player. The one thing he disliked about working Las Vegas, or any place that didn't happen to be in the Eastern time zone, was that he had to rise very early to call his bookie and place his bets for the day. (This was long before Las Vegas casinos had their own elaborate race and sports books.)

Lewis just didn't trust Las Vegas bookies: "You bet a few horses that don't happen to win and these guys are knocking on the door for their money. Can't they be decent and at least wait until the race is over?"

Helping Lewis through his roles as comedian and horse player was an acquired ability to consume vast amounts of alcoholic beverages. No one ever outdrank Joe E. Lewis. But even with a heavy load on, he held his liquor perfectly and actually had to fake the effects of the booze. It got to the point where Lewis would drink any time he was awake. It was even rumored that he set an alarm clock so he wouldn't miss a drink while he was sleeping.

One of Lewis' favorite leisure activities was to stretch out on a couch in his suite and watch old black-and-white horse operas on television. The original Hopalong Cassidy movies were his favorites. He also spent a fair amount of time visiting Austin Mack and his wife Cassie. Mack's wife served as critic, adviser, travel agent, and mother figure for the troupe as it traveled the country on a killer schedule, with only a few brief respites while Joe E. visited his favorite racetracks.

Swifty Morgan, a guy right out of the pages of humorist Damon Runyon, was another close friend of Lewis'. Morgan never showed any means of support other than the suitcase he always carried. In that valise was an assortment of perhaps 200 neckties, 100 pairs of cufflinks, a dozen watches, and various other pieces of jewelry, all for sale to anyone he could corner. Friends were his best customers and Joe E. was his best friend. After the great comedian passed on, you could have opened a menswear store with all the stuff he'd bought from Morgan.

Lewis was first, last, and always a player. He liked blackjack and especially craps, and his credit was always good. He wasn't a true casino gambler, preferring his horses. But he knew the games and how to lose.

Lewis was a great crowd-pleaser both on and off the stage. He would walk into the Flamingo casino, mosey into the pit, and tap a blackjack dealer on the shoulder, indicating that he wanted to take over the deal. He would start dealing the cards in a normal manner. Then, after delivering one of his own cards face up and the other face down, he would flip over his hole card and expose his hand, allowing the players to do their drawing or standing based on his actual score. If he happened to deal himself a natural, he'd either throw away the ace or trade it for a bad card from a player so the player would have a blackjack and his own hand would lose.

This same practice was adopted by Dean Martin, Frank Sinatra, and comedian Lou Costello during their early Las Vegas appearances. The guests loved it: It was fun and loose and they'd wind up winning a few more dollars. The casino owners loved it: Word of Lewis' antics spread and lots of people would hang around the casino after his show, hoping to catch an impromptu performance in the pit.

But stuck away in a warren in Carson City, the capital of Nevada, sat some obscure investigator for the state Gaming Control Board, the government agency that regulates gambling. This investigator determined that when an entertainer took over dealing cards in a casino, it violated all sorts of rules. The entertainer was not licensed by the county or state, he had no formal training as a dealer, and he wasn't employed by the casino. Most important, in exposing his hand to the players or paying off a losing hand, by gosh, he was *cheating*. This investigator recommended that the entertainers and the casinos be prosecuted for all violations.

Of course, this provided endless material for Lewis' monologues. But in the end, state authorities instructed the casino operators not to allow the entertainers to deal.

Las Vegas was growing up.

The Tears of a Clown

Shecky Greene has to be one of the funniest men ever to step on stage in Las Vegas. His style of stand-up packed the cocktail lounges at the Tropicana and the Riviera for three or four shows, seven nights a week, and sent audiences streaming into the casinos afterward holding their mid-sections from laughing so hard.

His audiences, however, never saw the other side of Shecky. He was a sad man who, for many years, found his only solace in a bottle. He loved and married a girl, then lost her because of his major mood swings. In addition, Shecky was a gambler. He played whatever games of chance were available. He was so well-known at the racetracks throughout the country that one horse owner named a thoroughbred after him. Unlike the man, "Shecky Greene" the horse was a consistent winner.

To top it all off, the gambling part of Shecky's schedule always followed the drinking part, when his faculties were not too sharp. Whenever he appeared in Las Vegas, it was a foregone conclusion that he would wind up working for little or no salary after paying off his gambling debts.

One evening, Greene, in a particularly melancholy mood, visited the Flamingo casino. He was drinking at a rate that worried even those who knew he had a huge capacity for liquor. Somehow, when the time came, he managed to make his way back to the Riviera, where he was scheduled to perform. People who caught his act that night insisted he was even funnier than usual.

Following his last show, Shecky took an elevator to his suite, changed into his pajamas, and pulled on a silk robe. Then he got back on the elevator and walked through the casino out into the parking lot. He climbed into his car, fired it up, and turned right onto the Strip, where he did a very strange thing: He maneuvered his car, facing north, into southbound traffic, and drove the mile and a half to the Flamingo—backwards. His car was pointing toward the Riviera the whole time, but he drove in reverse, keeping pace with the heavy flow of traffic, until he successfully backed into the Flamingo parking lot. A shocked parking attendant took over the vehicle.

After such a stunt, you might expect Shecky to be through for the evening. But he was just warming up. He re-entered the casino, apparently oblivious to the glances at his attire. Business was slow due to the lateness of the hour, but two dice games were still in progress. Greene walked purposefully toward one of the crap tables, where he stripped off his robe, climbed over the rail, and laid down atop the chips, dice, and cash. He placed the robe under his head as a pillow.

The dealers and players were almost frozen in shock. No one knew what to do. As usual, Chester Simms came to the rescue. He grabbed the comedian by one arm and dragged him to the edge of the table. At the same time, he called for assistance from the security guards and ordered someone to call the sheriff's office.

The burly Green was half-lifted and half-pulled from the table by a pair of beefy security officers and the determined casino manager. As the comic came off the table, all the chips, cash, and dice came with him, spilling onto the casino floor.

Chester Simms sat Greene down and was obviously trying to sober him up.

"I guess this means I'll have to go to my room, huh, Chester?" Shecky said to the casino boss.

"Yeah, Shecky, it's back to your room—for tonight, anyways."

Shortly, the cops showed up and escorted the chastened comedian to the county jail cell in which, now that he was having less and less success at keeping himself out of trouble, he was spending more and more time. So much time, in fact, that he'd begun referring to the cell as "my room."

A Closed Casino

There was only one time during my tenure at the Flamingo that no one found anything to laugh about. November 22, 1963, was such a beautiful day that as I drove to the Flamingo, I opened all the windows in my car, needing neither heat nor air-conditioning. Some of the nicest weather of the year comes to Las Vegas in November and this was one glorious morning.

When I got to the office, my secretary told me that Bonnie Gragson, the wife of Las Vegas' mayor, had called and wanted me to call her back. Bonnie was working on a big civic promotion that I'd offered to help with. I called and gave her a cheery greeting that wasn't returned.

"How can you even call me now?" she asked, on the verge of tears.

"Gosh, Bonnie. I'm sorry if I caught you at a bad time. I'll call back later." I was totally chagrined.

"Haven't you heard?" she blurted.

"Heard what?"

"The President's been shot."

I hadn't heard and neither had anyone in our office suite. No radios or televisions happened to be turned on. And the shooting had occurred mere minutes prior to my untimely phone call. I rushed over to Morris Lansburgh's office, only to find he hadn't come in yet. I was told he'd worked very late the previous night and was probably still asleep in his suite.

As much as I hated doing it, I asked one of the hotel operators to ring the suite. As feared, I awoke Lansburgh from a deep sleep. But after I told him the news, his normally booming voice was nearly a whisper. "I'll be right down," he muttered.

By the time he got to the office, Chester Simms was already there. We turned on the TV just in time to get confirmation that President Kennedy was dead.

Simms spoke first. "I want to close the casino right now."

Lansburgh and the rest of us who'd gathered were in agreement. But how do you close a casino that has no locks on the doors?

Simms had the answers. He picked up the phone and called the assistant casino manager. "Get all the dark green tablecloths you can find," Simms barked into the phone. "Use the tablecloths to cover every table game. Then turn all the slot machines so they face the wall. Tell Steve Delmont to get you as many tablecloths as he can and cover all the slots." Delmont had the cloths delivered within 20 minutes.

Pete Witcher, our chief of security, got on the phone next. After talking to his assistant, he hung up and announced, "I've rescheduled my staff so we'll have guards at all the doors for as long as you need them."

"I suggest we keep the casino closed until about eight o'clock tomorrow morning," Lansburgh, wide awake, added. "Also, we'd better cancel tonight's shows in the showroom and the lounge." He shuddered. "It's going to be awfully expensive, but we'd better plan on doing the same thing on the day of the funeral. I'll explain it all to the partners."

I then contacted the Las Vegas News Bureau, the publicity agency for the city and county, to explain what the Flamingo was doing to cope with a situation the likes of which had never been experienced in Las Vegas. It seemed that the other resorts were all doing the same thing. Within an hour, every casino in Las Vegas was still. It was absolutely eerie.

That evening, it got even stranger. All the hotels on the Strip and downtown turned off the huge garish neon signs and marquees. For the first and only time ever, Las Vegas was closed.

5

That's Entertainment

The Pre-Elvis Colonel

My job as entertainment columnist for the *Sun* took me one night to the new Sahara Hotel. This being its first year in business, the Sahara decided to celebrate Helldorado, Las Vegas' version of "pioneer" or "frontier" days, an event similar to that in every town of any size west of the Rockies. The casino was decorated with western artifacts and paraphernalia. Employees were encouraged to wear western shirts, jeans, cowboy boots, even beards. Singer Eddy Arnold was booked into the showroom.

That whole day, I'd heard Eddy Arnold songs, Eddy Arnold interviews, and Eddy Arnold commercials on the radio. Eddy Arnold interviews and ads filled the newspapers. I'd seen him walk through the *Sun* to have his picture taken. He was accompanied by a dapper Southern gentleman with a white mustache. It was the first time I'd laid eyes on Colonel Tom Parker.

Parker, who gained his greatest fame as the discoverer and manager of Elvis Presley, was Eddy Arnold's manager.

Even then, early in his career, the Colonel was a master showman.

He arrived in Las Vegas three or four days prior to Arnold's opening and visited newspaper offices and radio stations, always carrying pocketfuls of string ties, garters, pins, belt buckles, and other souvenir items—all bearing the name of his client. The Colonel also had his own way of introducing himself. He would walk up to a stranger and ask, "Have you met Colonel Tom Parker?"

When the stranger admitted he'd never had the pleasure, Parker would stick out his hand for a shake and say, "Well, you have now." It worked on everyone, from working men to royalty, throughout his career.

When Eddy Arnold arrived in Las Vegas, the Colonel whisked him around town, maximizing every opportunity for an interview. By the time the Colonel was through, the only Las Vegans who didn't know Eddy Arnold was appearing at the Sahara were deep in one of the mines that dotted the outskirts of town.

Arnold, the top western vocalist of his day, packed the showroom for the eight o'clock dinner show and the midnight late show. He was so popular that even his third show on Saturday night sold out.

I dropped by the Sahara after the third show to get the story and to collect some color about Helldorado. I happened to spot Sahara owner Milton Prell and his entertainment director, Stan Irwin, seated in the coffee shop. I asked what they thought of their western booking so far.

Irwin, always bright and cheerful, announced: "Eddy Arnold has set a new record for —"

"Yeah," Prell interrupted. "We've sold more beer in a single week than any hotel in Las Vegas history."

Mack the Knife

Then there was Bobby Darin, who never needed any advance man to work the town into a lather. A consummate entertainer, Darin was blessed with a great set of pipes and a perfect ear for music, but little in the way of patience. In the early 1960s, he was a regular at the Flamingo, appearing three or four times a year. He drew large crowds and had an amazing capacity to attract everyone from high-rolling gamblers to teenyboppers out for their first nightclub show.

Darin would step onstage and enthrall his audience every step of the way. He sang contemporary tunes as smoothly as he performed hits made popular during World War II and earlier. It was easy for him to segue from a jumpy version of "Splish Splash" into a plaintive love song, such as "Tenderly," which brought back bittersweet memories of the war to so many in his audience. Of course, every show ended with Darin's signature song, "Mack the Knife," which always drew a standing ovation from the packed showroom.

Bobby would then hustle back to his dressing room, which was crowded with friends, well-wishers, and a cadre of toads who lavished constant praise on the singer for anything he did. I sometimes wondered whether they sat with him while he was eating and told him how well he chewed his food.

Otherwise, Bobby Darin was a regular guy who, whenever he was in town, would stop by my office to shoot the breeze. A snapshot of him taken on opening night of one of his many appearances at the Flamingo by John Cook, a photographer from the Las Vegas News Bureau, hangs proudly on my office wall. When Bobby Darin was taken from us so early in his bright life, I felt I'd lost a good friend.

Little Fat Kids Grow Up

I never had anything against Wayne Newton. In the mid-'50s I'd watched Wayne and his brother Jerry go through their musical antics a few times in the lounge at the Fremont Hotel in downtown Las Vegas. Wayne was about 12 years old at the time and Jerry was maybe 14. In addition to playing a variety of musical instruments, Wayne did a little singing. His high-pitched voice sounded neither male nor female. It was best described as a Wayne Newton voice.

When comedian George Burns discovered Wayne and included him in some nightclub gigs, that was fine with me, too. And when Bobby Darin gave Wayne the song "Danke Shein" and Newton recorded his first hit record, good for him.

But when Morris Lansburgh called me into his office and told me he had just signed Wayne Newton to headline in our famed Flamingo Room, I was shocked. "You mean the little fat kid from the Fremont?" I asked disbelievingly. Lansburgh didn't even get a chance to answer.

Hershey Martin, one of the best talent agents in the business, who represented most of the top nightclub artists, broke in. "Not such a little fat kid any more," he boasted. "Wayne's doing turnaway business everywhere he appears."

Knowing that the booking meant a lot of money for Martin and the William Morris Agency where he was employed and that it would be my chore to prepare all the advertising, publicity, and promotional materials in an attempt to fill the showroom for the young man with the high-pitched voice, I remained skeptical.

Martin told us that Newton would be appearing at the old Coconut Grove in the Ambassador Hotel in Los Angeles the following week and invited me to come and see the new star in action. I agreed to go—but only because Lansburgh made it an order.

Martin had a table reserved for me toward the center of the room. I was startled to see so many middle-aged dowagers and so much blue- and purple-tinted gray hair. This couldn't be a Wayne Newton crowd. He might be a star among the teenybopper set, but certainly not for the Beverly Hills crowd.

While still trying to figure this out, I heard a voice off in the distance. As it drew closer, I recognized it as the voice of Wayne—there was no mistaking that—and accompanying the voice's arrival was spontaneous applause. Then, as Newton appeared and strolled toward the stage singing "Red Roses for A Blue Lady," women stood, reached out, and tried to touch him. I thought I'd suddenly been transported into the Twilight Zone.

The audience gave Newton a standing ovation before he even reached the stage. I proceeded to sit through a delightful hour of some of the greatest showmanship I'd ever witnessed. This young man had the audience in a frenzy throughout the show. When it came time for him to exit, it took several encores, followed by a final dropping of the curtain and raising of the houselights, to convince the yelling and clapping audience that the show was over.

Hershey Martin came to my table and sat down. "What do you think now?" he asked with an I-told-you-so smirk on his face. I conceded my amazement and told him I could now see my job would be a lot easier than I'd thought.

Martin then took me backstage to meet the star. The dressing room was jammed with admirers. Martin pushed through the crowd, grabbed Newton, and ushered him over toward the door where I was trying to stand out of the way. Martin introduced us and Wayne asked, "Well, what do you think of the little fat kid now?" We had a good laugh—mine while wearing a red face—and launched a great relationship.

Newton was probably the most cooperative entertainer I ever worked with. He especially enjoyed his appearances in Las Vegas, where he lived. He once told me, "It's great to come here to the hotel, entertain all those well-dressed folks, mix with them after the shows, then go home and sleep in the same bed I've had since I was a kid."

Onstage, Wayne Newton was a meticulously outfitted handsome young man, with every hair on his head in place and, when he chose to grow it, a perfect pencil-thin mustache. Offstage, so far as I recall, I never saw Wayne in anything other than Levis and cowboy boots.

During the years that Newton worked for us at the Flamingo, he was a virtual cinch to volunteer for every and any local charity that asked for his assistance. Since then, he's performed at all the leading Las Vegas resorts, in addition to making numerous appearances at his theater in Branson, Missouri.

And if you've ever wondered how old he is, Wayne Newton is exactly nine years younger than I am. We share the same birthday: April 3.

Good Old Prices

In the old days, when Eddy Arnold was a great star, Bobby Darin was alive, and Wayne Newton was a little kid, a 50-cent bottle of beer or a 25-cent cup of coffee was all you had to buy to catch the showroom performances of entertainers earning $50,000 a week or more. In truth, if you didn't want a drink, that was okay, too. Or you could opt for dinner during the show. In the Copa Room at the old Sands (now the Venetian), you and your date could enjoy a cocktail or two, a lavish New York steak dinner, and a 90-minute show that began with a full chorus line of beautiful dancers, followed by a well-known singer or comedian as the opening act, then ended with a star of the magnitude of Frank Sinatra, Dean Martin, or Sammy Davis Jr. Some nights, Sinatra, Dino, Sammy, and the rest of the Rat Pack would trot onstage together and treat the guests to a night they'd never forget. For all of this, you could pay the check, taxes, and tip and still get change from a $10 bill.

At the same time, stars such as Louis Prima and Keely Smith, Harry James, Joe Williams, Ray Charles, Lionel Hampton, Shecky Greene, Fats Domino, Della Reese, the Mary Kaye Trio, or Don Rickles might be appearing in the lounge of one of the resorts, playing three or four shows nightly. The lounges literally opened into the casinos and there was never a cover charge or drink minimum for the shows.

Those were the days when first-class hotel rooms went for as little as $5 per night for as many as four guests in a room. Indeed, a handful of these rooms are still standing at some of the older Strip resorts today and command rates of $45 to $60 per night. Old-timers often joke that some of these rooms are held up only by the many coats of paint the walls have received over a period of more than 40 years.

Then there was the original chuckwagon dinner served in most Strip hotels after 11 p.m., cost $1-$1.25. The modern-day Las Vegas buffets are an excellent value, but they can't compare with the lavish spreads—a table full of salads, prime rib sliced to order, fresh crab and shrimp galore, imported caviar, and obscene desserts—that were practically given away back then.

Bad New Prices

Shortly after the state of Nevada revised its gaming regulations to grant gaming licenses to public corporations, the legalized gambling industry changed forever, and so did the prices.

Prior to the era of Howard Hughes, who in 1967 duped the Nevada Legislature into allowing public corporations to own casinos, gaming licenses could be held only by individuals, who were personally responsible for anything that went on within their properties. That's why public corporations were prohibited: Every one of their thousands of shareholders would have had to be licensed individually. But Hughes changed all that.

Within a couple of years, the first publicly owned corporations appeared on the scene. They found that they'd walked into a philosophy of business that was completely foreign to them. The Las Vegas resorts tended to defy all the accepted rules of business practice. Virtually all guest-services departments were run at a loss. Only the huge revenues from the casinos kept the resorts profitable. In essence, Las Vegas was made up of a group of casinos — which happened to have rooms, restaurants, and showrooms attached.

This, of course, was not the way things were done by the hotel industry. The corporations wanted the rooms and restaurants to be profit centers of their own. They set about converting Las Vegas into a collection of very large resorts — which happened to have casinos attached. The corporate tycoons now insist on seeing suitable profits generated by every department, or heads would roll. *Casino* profits today are icing on the cake.

Anyway, when the corporations showed up everything changed, with little or no warning to the unsuspecting guests. The room they rented a year earlier for $12 was now $25. The chuckwagon was gone. In its place you could get a buffet breakfast for $1.95: no caviar, no prime rib, and no crab, just scrambled eggs, link sausage, and if you were lucky, fresh-squeezed orange juice.

In the showroom, guests found they paid for dinner whether they wanted it or not and the price was now $20 per person. The headliner policy, to be sure, was designed to lose money. To attract players, big-name entertainers were signed by bosses who knew that the good players comped into the showroom would stay and gamble afterward. But finally the stars' salaries got out of hand. When entertainers who were happy to earn a few thousand dollars a week on other stages around the country started demanding—and getting—$100,000 a week from the Las Vegas casinos, they literally priced themselves out of business.

Many hotels, like the Stardust and Tropicana, replaced their headliner policy with extravagant production shows, featuring scores of beautiful European dancers—including a sprinkling of nudes—spectacular costumes, some magnificent choreography, and a few vaudeville or specialty acts. These extravaganzas cost less to produce than paying for headliners. Best of all, the audiences loved them, filling up the showrooms twice nightly, three shows every Saturday.

From our vantage point today, even with inflated corporation prices, there were some pretty good deals. For example, *Siegfried & Roy*, who today perform to full houses at the Mirage at $90 a ticket, used to be the closing act in the Stardust's *Lido de Paris*, when admission and dinner cost less than $25 per couple.

With corporations running the show, the Las Vegas entertainment picture changed. No longer did the Las Vegas News Bureau advertise its town as the Entertainment

Capital of the World, because it simply wasn't so. A few hotels maintained star policies, but many others brought in production shows that cost less than the big extravaganzas, let alone that of a star. Today, only a few of the largest hotels book the old-time headliners, and then only on an occasional basis.

On the other hand, the prices of the most expensive production shows, such as *Siegfried & Roy, EFX, Folies Bergere,* and *Mystere,* could actually be considered bargains, even at $60 to $90 a ticket. These shows provide a type of entertainment that can't be found anywhere else in the world at any cost.

In addition, the biggest rock 'n' roll stars, who in the '70s and '80s wouldn't be caught dead on a Las Vegas stage, now flock to the city's many concert venues, from the MGM Grand Arena to the Joint at the Hard Rock. And all the new megaresorts seem to be using entertainment as the lynchpin in their plans.

From where I sit, I can see a Las Vegas entertainment renaissance about to emerge.

6

The Promoters

Goffstein and Schiller

No matter what historians might say about Gus Greenbaum, under his stewardship the Flamingo wound up making more money than anyone had ever dreamed. The success of the Flamingo inspired mob bosses from all around the country to begin viewing Las Vegas as the promised land. And for years the Flamingo remained the home to the highest of the high rollers who came to town. The lion's share of the credit for attracting them had to go to Benny Goffstein and Abe Schiller.

Goffstein was a veteran of Cleveland's newspaper wars in the 1930s and '40s. The daily papers battled each other for greater circulation, which translated into higher advertising rates. Heads were broken, trucks were overturned, and mayhem was the rule rather than the exception. Benny held various titles in the circulation department, but he was best known as a head-breaker.

I can't recall Benny ever being accused of perpetrating any sort of physical violence after arriving in Las Vegas. In fact, he was just the opposite. He had a laugh that could shatter a shot glass and a glad hand that could shatter your shoulder. And Benny could drink with the best of them. During his time at the Flamingo, when Joe E. Lewis played in the showroom, the two men had some drinking bouts of legendary proportions. Benny kept up with Joe E. every time.

Whenever Goffstein dealt with current or prospective customers, he always let them set the pace. He might take them to dinner and wait for them to place their cocktail orders before he would even consider ordering a drink for himself. And if his guests stopped after one drink, so did Benny. If they continued to drink, he matched them. The man had amazing control of his alcoholic intake. Many people thought Benny was an alcoholic, but it wasn't true.

He could talk the talk and walk the walk with virtually every type of potential high-roller guest who might come along. Benny was as comfortable with kings as he was with hoods. His following of customers was as good as it got. When Benny joined his boss, Gus Greenbaum, at the failing Riviera, he went to his black book and called his players, informing them of his move. And they dutifully came to gamble at his new store.

His dream was to build his own joint, and in 1966 Goffstein opened the Four Queens Hotel and Casino in the heart of Glitter Gulch, as downtown Las Vegas has always been known by the locals. He named the hotel after his wife and three daughters.

Construction of the Four Queens brought Benny under some local suspicion. The night before the demolition crew was due to level the old drugstore, along with the other shops on the corner where he was building, a mysterious fire burned them all to the ground. Then, during construction, Benny decided he needed more land along Fremont

Street, so he tried to negotiate with the owner of the business next door, who wasn't especially eager to leave his property. Soon, another fire broke out during the night and the building abutting the Four Queens was gone. Goffstein bought the land.

But the third time wasn't the charm. When construction of the hotel was near completion, Goffstein determined that it would be handy to have parking facilities adjacent to his new hotel. Again he made offers to the property owners and was turned down, and again a couple of fires broke out, but they were both extinguished and resulted in only minor damage.

Goffstein opened the Four Queens without a parking structure, but the hotel-casino flourished anyway. Nearly 20 years later, long after Goffstein had passed on, the owners of the Four Queens bought all the real estate remaining on the block. They bought the city-owned parking garage next door and built a new tower, which nearly doubled the size of the hotel.

The second half of the Flamingo's mighty one-two public-relations punch was Abe Schiller, the Jewish cowboy. Born and raised in Detroit, Schiller grew up as a hustler. Once he was old enough to protect himself and his merchandise, he started peddling jewelry on the streets and door to door. His following of customers, who liked his merchandise and low prices, included a few wise guys in the area. Abe caught the eye of some underworld bosses, primarily because of his great sense of humor and ability to get along with everyone, especially children. Most of the old-time gamblers were family men, but that was as far as their enjoyment of children went. Schiller, however, was a lifelong bachelor who loved kids.

When some of his customers and friends headed for Las Vegas where they'd bought into the El Rancho Vegas, they

brought Schiller along. Abe took to the desert, but kept trying to figure out what he could do to earn the paychecks
his pals were giving him every week. He finally decided
that his strength was in how he got along with people. So
he let his owner friends know that he would become the
public-relations department of the hotel.

Although he didn't exactly know what the duties of a
public-relations person were, Abe continued to hang around
the casino, greeting guests. A losing crapshooter himself,
he found it easy and natural to commiserate with losers.
Soon, newspaper reporters and columnists were going to
Abe when they wanted information about the property. He
handled such requests by passing them along to the head
of respective department head, who answered the questions.
But Abe always tagged along, learning the answers for himself and shmoozing the reporters and photographers, buying them lunch and figuring out how to get more of their
attention.

Abe's on-the-job training paid off. When Ben Siegel
opened the Flamingo in 1946, he hired Schiller, Hank
Greenspun, and Paul Price as his public-relations men.
Greenspun, who went on to become owner and publisher
of the *Las Vegas Sun,* and Price, who'd been a columnist for
the *Los Angeles Daily News,* both knew their business and
launched one of the most successful publicity campaigns
ever seen.

But it was Schiller who made the big score. Abe had
met and entertained a reporter and photographer from *Life*
magazine when they'd been in Las Vegas to cover some
story or other. Schiller still had their business cards, so he
called the reporter and told him about the Flamingo and
the great photographic possibilities of the "Star of the
Desert." The three-page photo spread in *Life* was probably
the most important publicity the Flamingo could have re-

ceived. This was during the era when *Life* was the most popular magazine in the world.

As he began feeling more comfortable in his PR position at the Flamingo, he traveled for the hotel. He went to Texas and hung out with oilmen who were big gamblers at the Flamingo. Then he started attending golf tournaments, because they were among the first sporting events to be televised. The television cameras gave him an idea.

Schiller wasn't readily distinguishable in a crowd. He stood about six feet tall and was fairly heavy. To attract the attention of the TV cameras to himself and the hotel, he decided to become a cowboy. He traveled to Los Angeles and met with a man who designed outfits for many of the actors who starred in western movies. Abe especially wanted a shirt, but this shirt had to tell a story.

Schiller contacted one of his oilmen friends and asked for some photographs of oil wells and an illustration of the earth in an oilfield, which showed the variety of soils and rocks that led down to a pool of oil. He took the graphics to the tailor, who made the shirt using sequins to provide all the colors for the soil, rocks, oil well and — of course — flamingos. This shirt, with Schiller wearing it for all of his out-of-town visits, became famous.

Next, he went to see the top brass of Justin Boots, which immediately became his bootmaker. Abe's boots were all specially designed and crafted out of all sorts of exotic skins, including ostrich, shark, and alligator. Schiller began getting invited to more and more western events and his wardrobe had to fit. So he went back to his tailor, with suggested designs for two more shirts and a cowboy tuxedo.

Over the years, Schiller had plenty of girlfriends, some of whom became live-ins. One young lady started talking marriage, but Abe kept changing the subject. This went on for several weeks, until it was time for him to head out for another western appearance. He promised the lady they'd continue the discussion when he returned, but apparently she didn't believe him. When he got back to Las Vegas, she'd moved out of his apartment. But before leaving, she'd taken a large pair of shears and cut up every suit, jacket, pair of slacks, tie, and even socks in his closet, and piled them in a heap in the bedroom. She also walked off with his cufflinks.

Abe was limited to the few western outfits still in his suitcase. He was now wearing the same getups every day out of necessity. His bosses liked the western wear and so did the guests; children followed him around like the Pied Piper. So he called his tailor and put in a rush order for two dozen more shirts, western-cut suits, and cowboy tuxedos. Then he called his friends at Justin Boots and put them in touch with his tailor, so they could supply a different pair of boots for each shirt. The custom shirts alone cost at least $1,000 apiece; some of the outfits ran close to $5,000. His transformation from street hustler to Jewish cowboy was complete.

Schiller loved all kinds of sports, but he was a rabid pro football fan. It got to the point where he rarely missed traveling to an NFL game every Sunday. He already knew a lot of the press people who covered the games and he became a familiar sight in the press boxes at stadiums throughout the country. Many players were attracted to Abe because of his colorful costumes, and some great friendships developed once the players became aware of Abe's fanatical interest and knowledge of football. In those days, the annual Pro Bowl was played in Los Angeles and Abe would entertain virtually every player at the Flamingo in conjunction with the game. He regaled them with banquets and shows, took them out on the Flamingo's fishing cruiser at Lake Mead, and treated them like the heroes he felt they were.

This went on until then-NFL Commissioner Pete Rozelle

informed all players in the National Football League that they were forbidden from associating with known gamblers. In fact, Rozelle actually mentioned Schiller by name; he declared that the Vegas cowboy was no longer welcome in the press boxes, in the dressing rooms, or on the sidelines at any NFL game.

This stung Schiller. I'd never known him to even make a friendly bet on a game, let alone try to influence a contest, but Schiller understood Rozelle's position. Hundreds of millions of dollars are bet on professional football games every week and Rozelle feared any possible chink in the armor of propriety. After all, Schiller wasn't just associated with Las Vegas; he was employed by a casino.

Still, Abe wasn't about to give up his love for pro football. He had a bank of six TV sets installed in his apartment so he could watch one or more games at a time. Then he contacted some of his friends who'd established the NFL Alumni Association, made up of former players from the league. He talked them into holding their annual meeting at the Flamingo, and later at the Dunes when Schiller moved there. During the closing banquet at one year's meeting, Schiller got up to make a speech. About halfway through his remarks, Abe slowly collapsed to the floor. The doctors said he was gone, from a heart attack, before he started to fall.

He had a smile on his face.

Party Time

Herb McDonald was another of the fabled few who performed the PR magic that helped put Las Vegas on the map. McDonald was a young eager press agent when Milton

Prell tore down his old Club Bingo to make way for the Sahara Hotel. He stayed at the Sahara for more than 20 years, spreading the name of the resort to every corner of the planet.

McDonald became something of a legend in the Las Vegas resort industry when he dreamed up a promotion known as the International Airlines Party. It was held in December, which attracted people to town during the slowest month of the year (then as now). Also, because it was a huge party for the employees of recognized airlines, thousands of people showed up, most of them making their first trip to Las Vegas. McDonald and his staff worked around the clock to ensure that everyone was favorably impressed by all the events; there was a continuous round of parties and special events for those who attended. When they got back to work, thousands of airline employees would spread the word on Las Vegas to millions of travelers every year.

The International Airlines Party was such a success that I paid McDonald the "sincerest form of flattery" when I patterned my International Press Christmas Party (described in Chapter Two) after his inspirational idea.

Murphy the Magnificent

One of the earliest and brightest public-relations experts to land in Las Vegas was also one of the most unlikely men anyone would expect to find in this land of make-believe. Eugene Murphy was a bookish intellectual fellow. His favorite pastimes were solving the most difficult mind puzzles he could find and reading advanced books on medicine. Why medicine? He never said.

Murphy's vocabulary was studded with multi-syllabic

words rarely heard in normal conversation. One time, he used one of his obscure words in the presence of Al Freeman, his counterpart at the Sands Hotel. Freeman had his comeback at hand. "I looked that word up in the Webster's Unabridged Dictionary," he quipped, "and the definition said, 'see Eugene Murphy.'"

What made the studious Murphy appear even more out of place were the people he worked for at Wilbur Clark's Desert Inn. Clark himself started out as a hotel employee in San Diego, then worked his way up to bar owner. He came to Las Vegas in the late 1930s and bought into several casinos. After accumulating a grubstake of more than $1 million, he set out to build a new hotel-casino, Wilbur Clark's Desert Inn. He immediately ran out of money, at which point the legendary Morris "Moe" Dalitz, boss gambler from Ohio and Kentucky, moved in and helped finance the completion of the resort. Clark stayed on as part owner, as well as greeter, host, and most capable front man.

Dalitz and his partners, another set of "deez, dem, and doze" types, were the earliest developers of Las Vegas' modern gaming industry. Murphy did a magnificent job, not only of spreading the Desert Inn story all over the world, but also of helping his bosses make the transition from gangsters to executives. He argued that in Nevada they could operate openly, with no payoffs to crooked police or politicians, and earn profits that could be legitimately invested or donated. He convinced his bosses and other bosses that they should show their appreciation to the community.

He herded them to church or temple, depending on their religions, and made sure that each was a generous contributor to his own faith and to other places of worship in Las Vegas. He kept the Desert Inn at the vanguard of civic attempts to raise funds for worthwhile causes, and made his bosses into the most respectable citizens possible.

Murphy formed a Tent of the International Variety Club in Las Vegas. Its Variety School for Handicapped Children became one of the greatest facilities of its type in the country. Moe Dalitz, in fact, made the Variety Club his special project; no one knows how many millions of his own dollars went to the school, as well as to hospitals and other charities. A lot of financial support still comes from the Dalitz estate today.

In addition to getting positive press for his hotel, Murphy was also a master at keeping his bosses names *out* of print, unless he thought the newspaper or magazine story would somehow be beneficial to the Desert Inn. Partly because of his high intellect and partly because he was well-placed in public relations, Murphy had a definite knack for manipulating the press.

Writers would visit Las Vegas bent on basing their stories on the big-time underworld characters running the town. But then they'd run into Eugene Murphy and would leave with their heads filled with marvelous tales about how Dalitz had just bought a new van for the Variety Club, or Ruby Kolod had donated the money to build a community swimming pool in memory of his son. Murphy was always able to establish order out of chaos, even though some of his Desert Inn bosses were masters of chaos.

Murphy played a major part in formulating the great Tournament of Champions golf event held annually at the Desert Inn Country Club. And he put together the deal that made the Damon Runyon Cancer Fund the recipient of many thousands of dollars raised through the tournament.

Most remarkable about Murphy, however, considering all his great abilities, was that he was a cold private man who found it difficult to warm up to those who tried to befriend him, including the bosses he worked so hard for. Thus he was always a bit mysterious in whatever he did.

His most mysterious moment came after he'd served the Desert Inn faithfully for almost 15 years. One day Murphy was called into the office by Moe Dalitz. No one knows what was said within those four walls, but when Murphy came out, a security guard was waiting to escort him off the property.

Eugene Murphy would never speak of the apparent firing. Moe Dalitz, too, remained mute on the subject for the rest of his life.

Freeman the Amazing

The uncrowned king of Las Vegas publicists had to be Al Freeman, who began his local career at the brand-new Sands Hotel — and ended it there as well.

Freeman had been a high-priced New York press agent who gained publicity for his clients with an astonishing rate of success. When he arrived in Las Vegas, he performed the same magic for the Sands and ultimately for all of Las Vegas. His first trick was orchestrating the grand opening of the Sands. Planeloads of movie stars and members of the press were flown in to rub elbows with one of the greatest collections of high rollers the town had ever seen.

After the opening, Freeman never relaxed for a moment. He immediately made the Sands available to the hundreds of reporters, photographers, and even a few TV crews that came to Las Vegas to cover the Atomic Energy Commission's series of atom bomb tests in the Frenchman's Flat area of the Mojave Desert, about 60 miles northwest of Las Vegas. Once he'd booked enough press into the Sands, Freeman pronounced the hotel the "official press headquarters" for the bomb tests. The military and government agencies involved fell for his declaration and scheduled all their press briefings and conferences there, garnering an enormous amount of publicity for the property.

Over the years, Freeman managed to keep the Sands before the local, national, and international press on a continual basis. One example was his design for a float for the annual Helldorado Parade. Most hotels participated in the parade and other Helldorado activities, but the Sands again ran off with all the newspaper space.

The float was a complete swimming pool, surrounded by the beautiful, leggy, buxom Copa Girls, the dancers and showgirls from the Sands' famous Copa Room. All the other hotel owners liked the float so much that the Sands name was removed and the float appeared in the Tournament of Roses Parade in Pasadena that year as the official Las Vegas entry.

Perhaps Freeman's most famous publicity stunt was a photograph he set up. He put a crap table in the middle of the Sands' swimming pool, again surrounded by the legendary Copa Girls. He captioned the photo, "The Original Floating Crap Game." This stunning Las Vegas image was picked up by the wire services and the picture appeared in thousands of newspapers all over the world.

But Freeman's most noteworthy accomplishment never drew any publicity at all for him or for the Sands. He and the Desert Inn's Eugene Murphy came up with the idea of establishing the Las Vegas Charities Foundation, a joint venture of all the local gaming resorts. The purpose of the foundation was to pay off the mortgages of all the religious institutions in town. Its vehicle was an annual gin rummy tournament. Participants ante'd up big entry fees and competed for major cash prizes. However, the prize money didn't come from the entry fees; the hotels put up the funds in a separate pot.

The tournament drew thousands of entrants from every corner of the world, so the Las Vegas Charities Foundation wound up with hundreds of thousands of dollars in entry fees. All proceeds collected were used to pay off the debts of all the churches and synagogues in Clark County. It took five or six years to pay off every mortgage. Once the goal was met, the Foundation was disbanded and the gin rummy tournament became another piece of Las Vegas history.

The Mad Genius

Jay Sarno was a man specially made for Las Vegas. He was a short highly volatile man who threw off showers of sparks wherever he traveled. A bundle of energy and a wild crapshooter, Sarno popped onto the Las Vegas scene in the early '60s after gaining a measure of fame in the resort world as an irrepressible promoter who usually turned up winners. He was fresh from a measure of success promoting a hotel in Texas with oilman Glen McCarthy when he arrived in town. The Texas endeavor hadn't made the Las Vegas press, so at first Sarno was just another crapshooter—a bit louder and more boisterous than most.

Sarno brought with him yet another promoter, Nate Jacobson, plus a fair amount of cash raised from a group of wealthy Texans who were impressed with Sarno's and Jacobson's refusal to conform to normal business practices and tactics—in the service of success. Most important, the pair brought with them wild plans for a Roman-themed casino-resort, the likes of which had never been seen anywhere in the world, let alone in the middle of the Mojave Desert.

To succeed with their dream hotel, they believed it necessary to build close to already established and successful properties. However, the price of the land for their proposed project had to be low. Although they were working from a bankroll larger than had been needed to build any Las Vegas resort to date, the developers had so much money committed to expensive materials, high-class furnishings, and fine artwork that they had to rein in the budget in other places, like land.

They eyed the intersection of Flamingo Road and the Strip, already shared by the Flamingo and Dunes hotels. Though worried that the price of the land would be out of their reach, Sarno decided to pursue the parcel: "What can they do but say no?" To his amazement, he found that the price was reasonable, considering its enviable location.

The landowner, a young speculator named Kirk Kerkorian, leveled with them, explaining that he'd bought the land at a bargain price because of the dry wash that ran across the property. Of course, he further explained, the wash rarely ran water through the property, only after extremely heavy rains.

Kerkorian was telling Sarno and Jacobson the truth: It was rare that the wash ever ran. However, the fact that it could, and did, had scared off numerous prospective buyers, including the owners of the Flamingo, who knew the wash better than most since it bordered their property. Still, Sarno and Jacobson moved forward. They altered the building plans so the hotel would be on the edge of the wash, instead of trying to build through the dangerous area, and began construction.

The name of the new property, "Caesars Palace," was enough to convince all the Las Vegas mavens that the place didn't stand a chance. "How do you sell a Roman orgy where Arab tents would be more the fashion?" asked a wise guy. Everything about the property was strange, including the marble, the statuary, giant fountains fronting the place, and an arc-shaped building bathed in blue light.

Even worse to some was the seeming assault on proper English when the possessive apostrophe was omitted from the word "Caesars." Though Sarno explained he wanted his grand resort to be "a palace for all Caesars," the local press changed every news release that came in from the hotel, adding the apostrophe to the offending word.

It wasn't until Sarno submitted "Caesars," without the apostrophe, for copyright protection that the scoffers realized that by using incorrect English, he could gain exclusive use of the name, while other hotels could not protect their names as they were simply common words or combinations thereof. Over the years, the copyright of the Caesars Palace name has enabled the resort to prevent all sorts of businesses from copying the name it has spent so many millions of dollars to promote.

But Sarno's diverse talents weren't limited to fooling around with the English language. He had bigger plans, and he sold his interest in Caesars for a hefty profit. With the proceeds, Sarno set about to build yet another hotel property that would be distinct in Las Vegas — or anywhere else in the world. And again, he started out with the unlikeliest name imaginable: "Circus Circus."

"What does it mean?" the same wise guy asked. Las Vegans and tourists alike wondered what variety of madman would try to combine a carnival midway, live circus acts, a resort-hotel, and a casino all under one roof.

Even the fact that Sarno had proved the skeptics wrong with Caesars Palace could not stop the tongue-clucking as the town — almost to a man — was certain Sarno would go broke with his project. This time, the naysayers weren't far from wrong — but not, as it turned out, for the reasons they originally imagined.

Sarno built his pink-and-white-striped "Big Top" casino and public areas, plus a handful of guest rooms. Everyone in Las Vegas turned out for the opening and some even risked a few bucks trying to win kewpie dolls and other prizes at the midway games. Players at the table games and slot machines on the first floor could look up at the ceiling and watch acrobats swinging back and forth over their heads. Most felt the activity away from the tables was a bit disconcerting.

After its grand opening, Circus Circus did not produce the mixture of business Sarno had predicted. One mistake he made was to charge admission to the carnival area, which prompted instant resentment from the community.

"We have to pay admission for our kids to go in and spend money to win a bunch of chintzy prizes," one father complained. "When is Sarno going to charge us admission to the casino for the privilege of losing our cash to him?"

The admission charge didn't last long, and soon the property had a little extra cash laying around. That's when Sarno's true love—shooting dice—came back into play. Whatever money entered the front door at Circus Circus seemed to find its way out the back door in the pockets of the owner to be squandered next door and put into the pockets of another owner.

In addition, once Sarno had accomplished his mission of getting another impossible idea off the ground, he began losing interest. But a pair of eager and able businessmen named Bill Bennett and Bill Pennington entered the picture—and a whole new story took shape.

Pennington, the owner of a slot machine business in Reno, and Bennett, the manager of Del Webb's Mint Hotel in downtown Las Vegas, learned that Sarno was looking for a way out of the business and they liked the looks of

Circus Circus. Not having the money to buy the place and uncertain about a future course for the property, Bennett and Pennington came up with an offer to lease Circus Circus and Sarno grabbed it.

Under the two young aggressive operators, Circus Circus' fortunes turned around. The partners cut excessive waste and began doing some heavy promotion to attract business. They never missed a lease payment and Sarno was always there to collect, so he could pay off his markers at other casinos. Within a relatively short time, Bennett and Pennington were able to buy the complex, which they transformed into one of the most successful operations in Las Vegas.

But Sarno was still not done. When he died in 1984, he was busy trying to raise the needed capital to build yet another casino based on a "wild" idea. His final plans called for a resort-hotel with more than 6,000 rooms. He boasted that, including employees, the hotel would be a city of 20,000, a fact nearly impossible to comprehend at the time. In light of the size of the MGM Grand and the Venetian, Sarno could actually have been an even greater visionary. than he's given credit for.

Las Vegas Works Together

You had to be there, in Las Vegas in 1955, to believe what happened during that one year.

First the Dunes Hotel opened at the corner of Flamingo and the Strip. A group of East Coast developers built their jewel of a property, then turned its operation over to Bill Miller, who had a string of highly successful clubs in New York and New Jersey and was probably the finest nightclub operator in the country at the time. Miller got his Las Vegas experience during the few years that he served as entertainment director for the Club Bingo and its successor, the Sahara. But running the Dunes was out of his league.

Soon after, the Hacienda, Riviera, Royal Nevada, and Moulin Rouge opened in quick succession. The Desert Spa was also supposed to join the fray, but it burned to the ground the night before the scheduled festivities. Each of these new resorts faced the same problem: They were competing with seven existing Strip properties, each with large loyal followings of customers.

The Dunes soon locked its front doors, unable to pay its bills or meet payroll. The Moulin Rouge also closed within the first few months. The Royal Nevada was sold to the owners of the Desert Inn; when the Stardust opened next to the Royal Nevada a couple of years later, it was managed by the DI's Moe Dalitz and crew, who ultimately combined the operation of the two properties. The Riviera was sold to the Flamingo bosses for a very low price. The Hacienda muddled through, financed well enough to stay alive until the situation changed.

Meanwhile, every other hotel in town was also in trouble to some degree. The addition of the new hotels more than doubled the number of rooms available on the Strip. Price wars erupted and rooms were virtually being given away. Things got so out of hand that the state Legislature enacted a law against hotels or motels openly advertising room rates within Nevada. This meant that properties had to take down hastily erected signs, many of which had rates scrawled in chalk, making them easier to change. Suddenly, billboard companies in California were besieged by Las Vegas resorts that wanted to advertise their low prices.

The death knell sounded for many Las Vegas motels as well. Until 1955, motels lined Las Vegas Boulevard, Boulder Highway, and Fremont Street. But they, too, started disappearing, never to return to a dominant position again.

The situation went from bad to worse when the nation's press began reporting the impending demise of Las Vegas and legalized gambling. Every major newspaper, wire service, and radio network, and even a few fledgling TV stations, sent reporters here to "cover the funeral."

Finally, the members of the Las Vegas Promotional Committee, which included the public-relations directors of every major hotel in town, went to work. They had to address the problem behind the backs of their bosses, whose interests were focused solely on their own properties and the hell with everyone else. This wasn't the first time these PR men, mostly rugged individualists, operated outside the purview of their own properties and without discussing the situation with the men who paid their salaries.

The Promotional Committee spent long days and nights developing a program they believed would not only breathe life back into Las Vegas, but also bring millions of new visitors to town. When they were ready, they went back to their bosses and showed them the plan. Now it was up to the owners to sit down and work together to keep their properties alive.

The group of owners followed the committee's suggestion to contact all scheduled airlines in the United States, whether they served Las Vegas or not. The few already flying into McCarran Airport were urged to devote more flights, direct and non-stop, from major markets. The hotels also launched a cooperative advertising campaign with the airlines and sponsored cocktail parties around the country to introduce the new plans to the entire travel industry.

One region of the country that had poor air service to Las Vegas was the South. Millions of potential customers and herds of high rollers simply couldn't get from there to here. The hotel owners met with the executives of Delta and National Airlines, which served almost every important market in the South, from Florida to Texas. Other parts of the country were similarly addressed. This concerted effort to promote Las Vegas turned the situation around and saved the day.

The one other time that all of Las Vegas pitched in and worked closely together came during the gasoline shortage of 1973. Although historians have since determined that the shortage was a sham perpetrated by major oil companies to raise the retail price of gas by 200 percent, at the time, certain gas stations could sell fuel only on certain days of the week and some stations simply closed for the duration.

Las Vegas was hit especially hard. Southern California was the primary market for the resorts, with Los Angeles 280 miles away. In those days of eight-cylinder gas-guzzling Detroit-made automobiles, few cars could make the lengthy trip across the Mojave Desert on a single tank of gas; most people driving in from L.A. could get only as far as Barstow before filling up for the rest of the trip. But during the gasoline crisis, no one could be sure there'd be gas in Barstow. Las Vegas' southern California business literally dried up.

At the time, I was holding down the marketing director's post at the Stardust, where we'd just launched a national promotion offering visitors an ultra low-priced package, including airfare, room, show tickets, and other entertainment. Our package was doing a big job for us.

However, in the gambling business, how your competitor casinos are doing is critical to how your own casino is doing. Gamblers like to move around. If they start feeling unlucky in one casino, they'll head for another place to try to change their luck. All any casino could depend on was the fact that those guests staying in its hotel rooms would start and end the day where they slept. The remainder of the time, everyone counted on guests moving from casino to casino.

So the Stardust had plenty of customers flying in every day. However, during the gasoline situation, our neighboring hotels didn't have the guests to wander into our place. It became a one-way street: Our guests provided neighboring properties with some play, but we weren't getting any in return.

Al Sachs, then president of the Stardust, called me into his office to discuss how we could help produce more business for the entire town. The biggest problem we were facing, we realized, was that every Las Vegas resort owner or operator thought he was the only one who knew the right way to do things. That's why joint ventures were rare among casinos back then. By the time I left Sachs' office, we'd developed the germ of a plan.

I returned to my office and started making what seemed like thousands of phone calls. First I called local officials. Then I spoke with public officials in the three primary communities across the desert where motorists usually stopped for fuel: Baker, Barstow, and Victorville, California. For a reason I'll explain later, I also called a member of the state Public Utilities Commission, who owed me a favor.

Once I'd made all the preliminary contacts, I took my program to Sachs, who by then was willing to try just about anything. I asked him to call a meeting of top management from every hotel and casino in Las Vegas. At Sachs' invitation, a representative from every resort in town showed up.

I conducted the meeting and found an audience that was somewhat skeptical at first. One naysayer stood and announced that he had it "on good authority" that the energy crisis would end before the first of May. It was now February. There was an immediate buzz of optimism in the room, so I reacted quickly.

"That's great," I said. "Now we can all go back and lock up our places until May. If the gas shortage ends then, we can open up again. If not, we'll simply leave the doors locked."

That got the attention of the owners and operators, and suddenly everyone was anxious to solve the problem. So I laid out our plan, then asked every casino to provide at least one person and $5,000 to help me implement it. For the first time in my Las Vegas history, I saw every owner and operator in total agreement.

I had a meeting already set for that evening with the heads of the Las Vegas Service Station Owners Association. My committee crowded the room and the station owners were impressed by the "Who's Who" of the town's movers and shakers that greeted them. There, too, everyone agreed that something positive had to be done. By the time this meeting ended, the station owners had committed to working out a schedule whereby at least two gas stations would be open around the clock to serve tourists driving into or out of town.

Then the committee headed south 90 miles to Baker, the last bit of civilization southern California motorists would see before Las Vegas. Again, a schedule was worked out to guarantee at least one station was open around the clock to take care of motorists.

Next stop Barstow, the halfway mark on the boring drive from L.A., where the same deal was struck. Our final stop was Victorville, 90 miles from Los Angeles and the largest of the three gateway towns. We received the same promises there.

Right after the Victorville victory, I arranged a session with the Public Utilities Commission, which usually met monthly. But at the behest of some of the most influential businessmen and highest taxpayers in the state, the commissioners scheduled an emergency meeting—on a Sunday, no less. We flew to Carson City and worked for several hours to get a break of some sort from the PUC, with chairman Noel Clark aiding our cause.

The PUC had ordered all electric signage turned off for the duration of the crisis. Without the spectacular displays of millions of lightbulbs and hundreds of miles of neon tubing, Las Vegas could not be the city visitors from around the country were expecting when they got there. The PUC finally compromised and granted us permission to turn on all the signs from dark until midnight. But, we were warned, if one sign was found illuminated after midnight, it would all be shut down again.

Among those attending the meeting was the owner of a major advertising agency, whom I'd invited in the event we could get this last obstacle behind us. Before we flew back to Las Vegas, the ad man called his office and instructed the art department, which was standing by, to begin working on some newspaper ads and radio and TV commercials. By the time we returned, we were able to go directly to the agency office to check out some concepts for a blitz-type advertising campaign. Everything was in excellent shape.

Monday morning, back in Las Vegas, my secretary and I split a list of the marketing directors of all the Las Vegas properties. By the time we were through contacting them, we had promises from 40 highly placed executives to join us in a full blitz campaign beginning the next day. All 40 of us boarded a flight to Los Angeles Tuesday morning, then went by bus to a hotel where we'd reserved a meeting room. We quickly divvied up all of southern California, from the Mexican border to Santa Barbara, a distance of more than 200 miles.

Teams were dispatched to visit every newspaper office and radio and TV station to let the media know that Las Vegas was accessible and open for business. Every man and woman who made the "blitz" trip did a fantastic job and the media throughout southern California were completely covered by Wednesday afternoon. On Thursday morning, the advertising broke and everyone who read a newspaper, listened to a radio, or watched television suddenly knew that gasoline was ensured for any motorist who wanted to drive to Las Vegas, starting immediately.

We flew back to Las Vegas to plenty of praise. For the first time since the energy crisis had struck, the telephones in the room-reservations departments were ringing. In fact, the full-page newspaper ads and bright radio and TV spots had the phones ringing off the walls. It turned out to be one of the biggest business weekends in Las Vegas history, as everything went exactly as planned.

Even the lone detractor, who predicted that the crisis would be over in a few months, called to say that he could not believe the business his hotel and casino had done for the weekend. "If you ever come up with another promotion that will produce this kind of business, count me in for ten grand. It would be worth it."

7

Crime and Punishment

They Kept the Peace

Around 1950, after the Desert Inn had opened and the Las Vegas Strip had grown to five resort hotel-casinos, everyone agreed that the area should be policed by the Clark County Sheriff's Department. Each hotel had its own security force, which handled the majority of problems on the property. Still, the owners and operators of the swank clubs wanted a legal police agency standing by to provide backup if necessary.

In the early days, it rarely was. Back then, it was widely known that crimes of violence would not be tolerated within the limits of Clark County, in which Las Vegas is situated. The Clark County Sheriff's and Las Vegas Police departments were there primarily to handle traffic, domestic disputes, juvenile crime, and the occasional brawl. Murder, rape, robbery, burglary, and car theft were almost unknown.

The casino operators took care of maintaining the peace, since they usually heard about crimes being committed before the law-enforcement agencies did, and they were used to dispatching problems their own way. If a local punk happened to break the window of a grocery store and help himself to loose change and a six-pack of beer, someone in a casino would hear about it. Then a couple of burly hotel security officers would change into civilian clothes and pay the young man a visit. Only when a situation was more serious would the guards visit the perpetrator in full uniform. Treatment for small-time local offenders was generally a pretty severe beating, and perhaps a whipping with a leather belt. This was usually adequate punishment, as well as a strong deterrent for any friends of the offender who might be heading in the same direction.

Some crimes required more severe punishment. A cheating dealer, for example, would be taken into a casino office where his hands were smashed with a hammer, permanently disabling him from dealing cards or handling chips professionally. This practice ended during the great civil rights movement of the '60s, when one dealer complained to the police and the district attorney's office about his rights being violated by the casino that meted out the punishment. The hotel was cited. I know of no more hand-smashing after that.

But casino owners occasionally had to call on the cops for assistance, so Glen Jones, the Clark County sheriff at the time, promoted Ralph Lamb and Lloyd Bell from detectives to lieutenants and assigned them to the Strip. The two burly young officers both were from pioneer families, spoke with drawls, were rodeo cowboys, and were the epitome of small-town western lawmen.

The four Lamb brothers were known throughout the state as the toughest quartet of hombres around. They proved it every year at the Lamb family reunion in Caliente, about 100 miles northeast of Las Vegas, near the family ranch. Although it was never an officially scheduled event, the finale of the celebration came when the four brothers got into their annual fight. A Lamb-brother fight was the classic mean, dirty, no-rules, and no-mercy battle, with older brother Floyd almost always dispatching the younger siblings—much as he had since they were all boys.

Lieutenants Lamb and Bell were a pair of big, good-looking, soft-spoken men—either could have played the part of the Marlboro Man. But Bell was probably the more polished of the two. He'd spent more time in the city than Lamb, who'd led the ranch life for many years. And it was Bell who found it easier to part with his badge to re-enter the civilian and business worlds, while Lamb devoted many more years to law enforcement.

Needless to say, when either Ralph Lamb or Lloyd Bell spoke, everyone listened. The pair visited each resort property every night of the week. They would chat informally with the security guards, then sit down with an owner, general manager, or casino boss and review all sorts of situations. The cops would keep the managers apprised of new scam artists in town, hustlers and their hustles, particular prostitutes to be kept out of casinos, and whatever odds and ends happened to be on their minds.

In turn, the bosses provided the two lieutenants with information they could use, much of it concerning situations outside of Las Vegas the bosses thought might be headed their way.

It was a usual practice for Lamb and Bell to pick up troublemakers who came to town and, before they could cause problems, dispense a particular brand of justice that came to be known as "Nevada extradition." The procedure was simple. A phone call was made to California to find out whether any warrants were oustanding on the miscreant, which there usually were. They would then ask that a California Highway Patrol unit meet them 44 miles south of Las Vegas at the California state line. The bad guy would be driven into the desert and kicked out of the Clark County sheriff's car, where California authorities would take over.

Although this may not have complied with the letter of the law, it saved a tremendous amount of time, paperwork, and expense for all the agencies concerned. It also took a lot of punks off the street, instead of allowing them to continue preying on the public while the bureaucratic cogs and gears ground away. Most of these offenders were criminals on the run who seemed to think that Las Vegas would make a great place to hide. They didn't bank on the customs of local law enforcement, however, or on the bird-dogging talents of the two lieutenants who kept the Strip clean and safe for tourists.

Lloyd Bell left the Sheriff's Department and became a successful retailer in Las Vegas. Ralph Lamb went on to win several elections as sheriff of Clark County.

Russian Louie

During my first stretch in "Devil's Island with privileges," it was part of my job as the only full-time reporter for the *Las Vegas Sun* to personally visit both the sheriff and police chief every day. Each had a looseleaf binder, labeled "Press Book," on their desks. The press book was supposed to contain reports on any crime that occurred in their jurisdictions within the past 24 hours. I'd show up at the appointed time and the sheriff or chief of police would glance through the book before handing it to me. This is not to accuse them of practicing censorship, but I never found a single major incident in the binder.

One time I noticed a notation: "Russian Louie missing."

A well-known character in those days, "Russian Louie" was a gent who operated on the periphery as a moneylender, sometime bookmaker, and fast-buck artist. He must have crossed some line, because one day Louie's doorbell rang and he was seen getting into a car with two well-dressed gentlemen. At least they looked like gentlemen to the witness. Louie was never heard from again and his body was never found. However, a few days after his disappearance, a rumor went around that Louie flew in a private plane to Palm Springs with those same two gentlemen. While flying over the mountains, for some reason Louie decided he wanted to take a walk, so he opened the door and stepped out. The binder, of course, recorded only the fact that Louie was missing.

Probably the biggest crime committed along the Strip during my tenure at the *Sun* was an armed robbery of a bookmaking operation run out of the Flamingo Hotel. One afternoon after most of the horsetracks were closed, two tough-looking customers walked into the Flamingo book, pulled guns, and robbed the place of a couple hundred thousand dollars.

Even though I covered law enforcement at the time, I never heard a word about the incident, which naturally garnered no publicity. But shortly afterward, I walked into the office of Las Vegas Police Chief Al Kennedy to find a very angry lawman. I was surprised; Kennedy was usually a quiet and gentle guy. But this day he was hot.

"Have you heard about the two Tonys?" he barked.

I had no idea what he was talking about, and told him so.

"The two dummies who knocked over the Flamingo book the other day."

Something else I hadn't heard about.

He then explained that Tony Troncato and Tony Trombino, a pair of out-of-town hoods, had walked into the Flamingo racebook and robbed it of a lot of money.

Apparently the people at the Flamingo had learned the identity of the two gunmen and had people out looking for them. Someone asked the chief to intervene, explaining that the two hoods realized they'd made a terrible mistake and wanted to atone. Chief Kennedy visited with the Tonys, learned they still had the loot from the robbery, and convinced them that giving back the money was their only chance of staying alive.

From there, Chief Kennedy went into negotiations with the Flamingo to arrange the return of the money and allow the thieves safe departure from Las Vegas. He reported the terms to the Tonys and warned them to sit tight and not leave Clark County, where the underworld bosses wouldn't stand for any killings.

But the two Tonys were too smart for that, just as they'd figured they were smarter than the entire Miami underworld, which controlled the Flamingo.

Then I learned why the chief was so angry. He'd just gotten word that Troncato and Trombino had been discovered in Hollywood, seated in the front seat of a black Cadillac with their heads blown off. "I warned them!" Kennedy yelled. "But they knew everything. So now they're dead."

Another incident occurred during that same period. An old-time hood with all the proper connections was suspected of being a hidden owner at the new Sands Hotel. His name was Allen Smiley. He'd been born in Russia, though he'd lived in the U.S. since childhood. He was a good friend of Bugsy's — so good that he was sitting on the other end of the couch at Virginia Hill's Beverly Hills pad when Siegel got blown away.

The government wanted to deport Smiley, who'd allegedly violated most of the laws on the books regarding racketeering. But Smiley never went into hiding from the feds so far as I could tell. He had a ranch in northern California and a home near Phoenix. Once the Sands opened, he made regular drives from San Francisco to Las Vegas to Phoenix. When he reached Las Vegas, he would stay a few days at the Sands, then head on to Phoenix. Sometimes on his return from Arizona, he would stop over in Las Vegas again.

Once I mentioned in my column that Smiley had been in Vegas visiting his friends at the Sands. The following day, an urgent phone message from Salt Lake City awaited me at the newspaper office. I called the number and heard, "Good morning, Federal Bureau of Investigation." At that time, Las Vegas, which was supposedly crime-riddled, still wasn't big enough to rate an FBI office of its own, even though J. Edgar Hoover was a regular visitor to Moe Dalitz's Desert Inn.

I reached the agent who'd called and he told me that he'd read the item about Allen Smiley having been in Las Vegas. He wanted me to call and inform him the next time Smiley got to town, telling me what a bad guy he was and enumerating all the federal charges against him. In turn, I told him my job was to report news and his job was to catch bad guys. I suggested that the vast resources of the FBI should be sufficient to locate Smiley, especially since he didn't appear to be hiding from anyone.

Allen Smiley died peacefully during one of his visits to his Arizona place several years later. He was never even arrested by the FBI.

Torpedoes Away

Like some of the casino bosses, a pair of gangsters looked out for me. These were two men who, it turned out, were devoted fans of mine. One night, as I was strolling through the Sands, headed for the Garden Room restaurant, a man seated with another fellow in the lounge called to me. Though neither was at all familiar to me, I walked over to the table. I shook hands with them and they introduced themselves as Frankie and Paulie. They were right off the streets of New York. I could picture them standing on a street corner, hands pushed deep into their pants pockets, continously asking each other what they wanted to do.

Their first objective was to make sure I was who they thought I was. They picked up a copy of the *Sun* and compared the real me to the tiny photo at the top of my column.

"Yeah, that's you. You're Dick Odessky. We read your column every day. Boy, you know everything."

We chatted briefly and then I went on my way.

I soon learned that Frankie and Paulie were hit men. They didn't advertise it, but one of my contacts knew them and praised them as two of the best in the country. Every night I walked into the Sands, they would be seated at their usual table, reading the early edition of the *Sun*, always eager to ask me about various items I'd written.

Realizing that their business interests were quite limited, anytime I went to the Sands and didn't find Frankie and Paulie there, I said a silent prayer for whomever their latest victim might be.

One night, after going through our question-and-answer period, I continued on to the Garden Room, where I was to meet someone. Just after I was seated in my usual booth, an irate young man strode up to the table and began making it crystal clear that he was upset with me and probably wouldn't be satisfied until he had extracted a fair-sized chunk of my hide. I recognized him as a "production singer" for one of the shows on the Strip. (The production singer accompanied the chorus line through its routine and introduced the stars during the show. Most production singers were essentially anonymous. However, this one was regarded around town as quite a ladies man.) He was livid about an item I'd reported, regarding his current flame, a well-known dancer at another hotel.

He took great offense at the report, primarily because he was married. It was a fact he'd kept well hidden from everyone in Las Vegas, including me. This guy continued to harangue me for several minutes, until the next thing I knew, Frankie and Paulie had positioned themselves on either side of the guy.

Frankie looked over at me. "Some kinda problem here, Dick?" he asked in his soft voice.

The singer turned to him and yelled, "You bet there's a problem. I'm gonna *kill* this son of a bitch!"

"Hey, let's just calm down, friend," Frankie said. Now, anyone who knows anything about the kind of work people like Frankie and Paulie do never wants to hear the word "friend" or "pal," words that are usually reserved for their "business dealings." But this singer wasn't too sharp, and he continued yelling at them.

Paulie tried to quiet him down, without success. Finally, he said, "Maybe we ought to get you out of here so you can cool off a little." With that, the three men turned, the torpedoes still flanking the singer.

As I watched them go, I noticed that the singer's feet weren't touching the floor. Frankie and Paulie were actually carrying him out. I jumped up, caught up, and pleaded with my two acquaintances to let him go and forget about the matter. It wasn't important. But Frankie assured me they would "take care of it."

They left the Sands. I went back into the restaurant. My fears were great for the loud-mouthed singer, and I knew I couldn't leave until I found out what had happened. I tried to conduct business with the man who met me for dinner, but I was too preoccupied to concentrate. At that point, I was just waiting.

About an hour later, Frankie and Paulie returned. Noting the time, I knew they couldn't have driven into the California desert, disposed of the singer's body, and returned. I also knew they would never dump a body in Nevada, so that meant he was probably still breathing. Thank God. But what had happened? I rushed up to them and asked, and again was told that the guy just wanted to "cool off." Since it was mid-January and the desert is chilly at that time of year, I tried not to think what they meant by that.

I stayed at the Sands for another three hours. Just before five in the morning, I heard my name called over the paging system. I grabbed a house phone and identified myself. A few clicks later I heard the voice of the singer at the other end of the line.

"Before your friends dumped me, they made me promise to call you and apologize as soon as I got home." His voice was penitent. "But more than that, I want to thank you for sparing my life. They told me they would've killed me if you hadn't insisted they not do it. I really want to thank you." He was crying.

"Tell me," I broke in. "What the hell happened?"

"They drove me out to Blue Diamond on the dirt road. Then they pulled off the road, into the sand and cactus." I knew the area; it was about as desolate a spot as there was in southern Nevada, even though it was only about 10 miles from town.

"All the while, they kept debating whether to kill me or just hurt me bad. They were dead serious. I kept trying to apologize for whatever I said that got them so upset, but they wouldn't even listen." The singer was obviously reliving the experience in great anguish.

"They finally stopped the car and made me get out. It was so black, I couldn't see anything at all. Then one of them flicked on a small flashlight and guided me to a big cactus patch and told me to strip. The taller one even pulled a gun. I guess they wanted to be certain I took them seriously.

"I took off my shirt and pants and stood there," he continued. "The ox with the gun told me to take off everything. I wasn't about to argue, so I did. Man, it was freezing. And there were cactus needles poking into the bottoms of my feet.

"They took everything except one of my socks. They told me that should be enough to cover my big mouth, anyway. Then they drove off."

"Yes," I responded hurriedly. "Then what?"

"I stood in the middle of the damned desert and cried. I don't know whether it was from relief at not being killed or feeling sorry for myself because I was so damned cold. I must have stood there for a good ten minutes bawling. And I kept moving that one damned sock all over as I tried to keep warm.

"Somehow, I found my way back to the dirt road and started walking toward the highway. I didn't know what I'd do once I got there, wearing the single sock, but I had to get off that damned freezing desert. When I was about a hundred feet from the highway, a sheriff's car pulled off.

"When I told them what happened," he went on, "they laughed like hell. Apparently this type of thing isn't new in town. I only hope I never hear of it again. Anyway, after they had their laugh, they pulled a blanket out of the trunk of the car, threw it around me, and told me to hop in the back seat.

"Once in the car I looked down at my feet and saw they were bleeding where the cactus had cut into me. Otherwise,

I was turning a light blue from the cold."

Then he went on to relate how the cops had taken him to an all-night diner for some hot coffee, but made him get out of the car in his blanket so they could show him off to four other cops already parked there. Then they drove him home. The singer resumed his apologies and thanked me again for saving his life. He left town shortly afterward and I lost track of him.

Frankie and Paulie also left town, telling me they'd found some new work in Japan. I wished them well and said a prayer for the folks with whom they would be dealing in the future.

He Got Out the Hard Way

Gus Greenbaum. He and his wife were stabbed — their throats so deeply slit that they were nearly beheaded — in their home shortly after Greenbaum and his partners sold their interests in the Flamingo and bought the newly opened and struggling Riviera Hotel.

Greenbaum had been sent to Las Vegas to take over control of the Flamingo after Benjamin Siegel was blown away in Virginia Hill's apartment. Greenbaum was a no-nonsense individual; to me, he was the most frightening man I ever met or knew. He was of medium height and on the heavy side, with a face that would have intimidated most anyone. His dark deep-set eyes were flanked by high cheekbones that accented the depth of those eyes. His mouth turned downward and his jaw jutted at you almost like the end of a gun barrel. To top it off, Gus Greenbaum's personality was as dark as his physical being.

I was summoned to Greenbaum's office once during

my time as a reporter, and that one time was more than enough for me. I'd received a call from Abe Schiller, the Flamingo's public-relations director, who told me that Mr. Greenbaum wanted to see me. The invitation alone made me wonder whether I ought to leave town right then. But I was still macho enough to respond. I went to Greenbaum's office at the appointed time. There, I was met by Benny Goffstein, a bear of a man with a wonderful personality who didn't seem to belong with Greenbaum.

Benny ushered me into the office. The lights were turned down low. Greenbaum sat deep in his chair, nearly invisible behind the huge desk piled high with papers and assorted items. Benny told me that Mr. Greenbaum was building a brand-new landmark for Las Vegas. I thought I heard a grunt from the opposite side of the desk and then Greenbaum rose. He actually stuck out his hand and uttered something like, "Hello Dick." I wasn't sure.

He picked up an item from the desk—it resembled a silo—then reached across and turned on a light switch. The silo was suddenly ablaze in tiny light bulbs.

"This is my new 'Champagne Tower,'" Greenbaum proclaimed. "It stands eighty feet tall and these bubbles light from the ground upward. When they reach the top, other lights are triggered. They're so super-powered and bright that you'll be able to see this whole tower all the way from the border."

I certainly wasn't about to argue the point, even though the California border is more than 40 miles south, with a couple of mountain ranges and the curvature of the Earth blocking the way. If Gus Greenbaum said it, that was exactly how I'd report it, using his direct quote to make it clear that those were his words, not mine. The Champagne Tower, forever known as "the Silo" by locals, was built and put on a great light show for many years. But I never heard of anyone seeing it from the border. It was finally torn down in the early '70s by Hilton as part of its remodeling of the Flamingo.

After Greenbaum and his associates moved to the Riviera, he and his wife spent more time at a winter home they owned in Phoenix. It was only a matter of a few months before the headlines of newspapers all over the country screamed of the brutal slayings of the Greenbaums.

The murders have never been solved, and Las Vegas veterans never anticipated that there'd be an arrest or conviction. It was well-known that the horrible crime was carried out by professionals. Greenbaum had some very bad habits: heroin, gambling, and showgirls. It was rumored that he owed about a million dollars in markers to the Chicago mob, which then owned the Riviera. Also, his bosses at the Flamingo were irritated that he'd gone to work for the competition, taking all the hotel's secrets with him. The bloodiness of the killings (and the fact that Bess Greenbaum was taken out) seemed to indicate just how pissed off the boys were at Gus.

But true to the code, the murders didn't occur in Nevada.

Their strong-arm tactics were consistently rebuffed by Binion in Texas, so the Mob didn't bother Benny in Las Vegas. (Binion's Horseshoe Collection)

A young Jackie Gaughan (left), son of an Omaha bookmaker, with Ed Barrick, one of Gaughan's father's partners and a shrewd investor in Las Vegas desert scrub.

Sam (right) and Bill Boyd: one of several father-son Las Vegas casino owners.

The El Rancho Vegas, opened in 1941, was the first resort-casino
built to attract traffic off the Los Angeles Highway, soon to be known
as the Las Vegas Strip. (Manis Collection)

"Bugsy's safe" made for dramatic television—until it was discovered to be empty. (Las Vegas News Bureau)

Comedian Myron Cohen poses with the author (in rickshaw) for a Chinese New Year's promotion in the early 1960s.

Funnyman Joe E. Lewis was legendary for his hard drinking, as well as his gambling on the ponies. (Las Vegas News Bureau)

The "Jewish cowboy," Abe Schiller (right), with Jack Benny in front of the Flamingo's Champagne Tower, which locals dubbed "the Silo." (Las Vegas News Bureau)

Poolside at the original Desert Inn, opened in 1950. The second-floor Sky Room restaurant windows overlook it. (Manis Collection)

right (top): Desert Inn builder and Las Vegas elder statesman Moe Dalitz accepts a stuffed monkey at his 80th birthday party. (North Las Vegas Library Collection)

right (bottom): The Desert Inn's Wilbur Clark (right) hands a donation for the Damon Runyan Memorial Fund for Cancer Research to famous media personality Walter Winchell. (Wilbur Clark Collection)

Legendary Sands entertainment director Jack Entratter greets John F. Kennedy, at the time the U.S. senator from Massachusetts. The Kennedy assassination marked the only time in Las Vegas history that all the casinos closed simultaneously. (Sands Hotel Collection)

Sands boss Jake Freidman with actress Kim Novak in the Sands casino. (Sands Hotel Collection)

Snapshot of a casual Kirk Kerkorian, perennially near the top of the *Forbes 400* list of the richest people in the country.

High-powered gathering at a '60s' Stardust shindig. Back row L-R: Jay Sarno, Toni Clark, Hank Greenspun, Kirk Kerkorian. Front row L-R: Jean Kerkorian, Charlie Harrison, Joyce Sarno, Theda Harrison, Harold Ambler, Barbara Greenspun. (Wilbur Clark Collection)

(above): Stardust promo shot from the 1950s; notice the Las Vegas News Bureaumobile in the background.

(below): 1950s' aerial of the Stardust and the Royal Nevada. The Royal Nevada opened and closed in 1955 and was later merged into the Stardust. (both courtesy of the Stardust)

Allen Glick, president of Argent Corporation, was an unwitting front man for the Chicago mob. (North Las Vegas Library Collection)

Frank "Lefty" Rosenthal pulled Glick's strings; he managed to run the Stardust for several years without the benefit of a state-mandated key-employee license. (North Las Vegas Library Collection)

Hank and Barbara Greenspun took on the old-boy network, both statewide and nationally, in their newspaper, the *Las Vegas Sun*.

Valley Times publisher Bob Brown.

8

The Gamblers

He Lived Like a King or a Pauper

Few gamblers achieve legendary status, but there's one I'm sure almost everyone has heard of.

If this gambler came through the door freshly shaved, wearing his traditional dark pinstripe suit that had been pressed within the last half-hour, a starched white shirt, conservative necktie, polished shoes, and ever-present big black cigar, he was there to play.

If he walked in with a few days of whisker stubble, his pinstripe suit looking like he'd slept in it, and the shoes scuffed — but still smoking a big black cigar — he was there to mooch dollars, dimes, or nickels.

He was Nick the Greek, and whether he'd come to play or mooch, he was always puffing on that big black cigar.

Nicholas Dandolos was an experience for everyone who happened to catch this super high-roller in action, taking on a crap game, a poker table, or even some obscure proposition. He was also an experience for anyone he ever touched for a quarter or a dollar when his luck was bad. There was never a middle ground for the Greek. At any given time, he was either at the top or the bottom.

Dandolos was admired by gamblers of all stripes, who realized the Greek had a computer in his head thirty years before computers were invented. He could figure complex patterns of odds in an instant and always knew how to gain the greatest advantage in any game of chance.

The Greek's big problem was his inability to manage his finances. He was a plunger, both in gambling and life. At the tables, he turned into a merciless animal when the dice or the cards were working in his favor. And on those occasions when he walked away a winner, he was a *big* winner. Then he would be the most generous host who ever walked the earth, repaying his grubstakes with interest, buying expensive gifts for his friends, taking a dozen or more acquaintances to the highest-priced restaurants — generally living up to, and often beyond, his winnings.

Of course, as with any gambler, the Greek also had losing sessions at the tables. As affable and generous as he was when winning, Nick Dandolos was a miserable loser. During losing sessions you wouldn't even recognize him as the same man. He looked haggard and worn, his clothes suddenly ill-fitting; he coughed and moaned a lot and became a general pain in the neck.

One afternoon, while dropping thousands of dollars in a crap game at the Sands, the Greek hailed Carl Cohen, the casino manager and a true all-weather friend.

"Carl," he said, touching the boss on the forearm. "You don't need to use loaded dice to beat me. At least give me an even break."

A mild-mannered man, Cohen bristled at the accusation. Had it been made by someone else, Cohen might have reacted more strongly. But he knew the Greek and felt too sorry for the man to get angry with him. Instead, Cohen closed down the game and escorted Nick back to his suite.

Later, when the Greek returned to the casino, he'd obviously had some sleep and a shower, and came back in as the man the dealers loved. He immediately found Cohen and apologized for hurling the one accusation that is not made in polite gambling company. Then he strolled around until deciding to move in on another game of craps. This time the dice were smiling and the Greek walked away a big winner, happy with the world.

Later that same night, he decided to play a little more before turning in. He lost back all his winnings, plus the remainder of his original stake. Carl Cohen had left hours ago, so shift manager Bucky Harris had to absorb the abuse. It was a common series of events for the Greek.

With even a marginal program of everyday money management, Nick might have wound up a wealthy man. Instead, he lived from hand to mouth, never sure where he would be sleeping the following night.

When he was tapped, he would hit up anyone he knew in Las Vegas for whatever money he could get for "car fare." That amounted to a plane ticket to Los Angeles and a stake to get into the poker games in the Gardena card clubs. Once he got a few hundred dollars together, he was off to the airport. Within a matter of days he'd return to Las Vegas with several thousand dollars he'd taken from poker players who thought they could stand up to Nick the Greek.

Had money alone been his goal, the Greek could have fleeced poker players in the cardrooms of Gardena or in the high-stakes games played around the country. But his desire was to be recognized as the biggest gambler in the world and he could never gain that notoriety simply by winning money. Everything had to be done with style and panache.

So it was back to the big game, the high-stakes high-glamour action of Glitter Gulch. This is where the Greek was at the top of his form, where he put on his best show. The dice were his true love, but they were also his nemesis: He knew the odds were always against him, so he sought every possible advantage he could scratch and claw—legitimate or otherwise. He would see some minuscule opportunity, some pinhole of an opening, and in he'd jump to bluster or badger a winning bet out of the joint.

He would accuse the house of not getting a winning bet down; of shortchanging him on a bet payoff; of allowing the dice to roll to a losing seven without bouncing off the backboard; of switching dice in the middle of a hot roll. Life was a big poker game that he never stopped playing, and he loved to bluff—especially when he'd already lost the bet and stood only to turn it into a winner.

He wasn't above more elaborate cons, either. In the 1940s a Greek family owned a small casino in downtown Las Vegas. Because they were from the same country, Dandolos and the casino owners became friends. Or at least the owners thought this was the basis for their relationship with Nick the Greek.

Dandolos, however, looked at things differently. One time, after a losing crap marathon, he stopped in for some consolation from his new friends from the old country. He cried the blues as only the Greek knew how. This went on for more than a day, during which time his countrymen housed and fed him. But the Greek was after bigger game, so he changed his tack. He convinced his hosts he'd make their casino famous by playing there. The only problem, ahem, was that he didn't have a dollar in his pocket.

He asked for a line of credit. How could they turn down a fellow Greek? The casino owners extended him a load of chips, which he gambled and lost at their crap table. He pleaded for more credit, which he received, promising to pay off his markers the minute he got to his Los Angeles bank. Another bluff.

The Greek continued to lose and continued to sign markers, till he owed in the mid-five digits. Finally the dice turned and he proceeded to go on a tear in which he recouped his losses, then went for blood. It lasted for two days—no sleep, no food, only short breaks to run to and from the john. He turned into a shark finishing off a wounded prey, and he didn't stop until he'd ripped all the flesh from its bones.

When it was over, the casino operators had to give up. Nick the Greek had broken the bank. Now all he cared about was collecting his winnings and being on his way to another casino that still had cash in its vault.

His countrymen had to take a large emergency loan to cover the Greek's winnings and, within a few months, were forced to sell out when they couldn't repay the money.

The Greek? He hopped into a cab and headed for the Strip, where he lost every dollar at another crap table. But he wasn't through yet. He telephoned his former friends and asked if they might be able to lend him car fare to get to Los Angeles.

Father Bilko

A San Francisco man who attracted a great deal of attention from the casinos was a Catholic priest who ran a boarding school for youngsters in a small town just north of Baghdad by the Bay. He was said to have come from a wealthy family and used a large part of his personal fortune to support the school.

When he began visiting Las Vegas, it was to raise funds to help support the school. He targeted the casino bosses and point holders, rubbing shoulders with the managers and owners with ease and grace. He would sit down over a cup of coffee during the day or a glass of wine at night and show them brochures and photographs of his school. Evidence of his involvement in the school was apparent from the snapshots, in which he could be seen teaching in a classroom, leading services in the chapel, or just romping with the kids. His piety shone through the photographs, as did his love of fun.

At one point, a hotel general manager offered to sponsor a fundraising dinner for the school. The clergyman thanked him profusely, but insisted that he didn't want it ever to appear he needed any outside assistance in supporting the cause. Noble spirit that he was, he wanted to support the school from his personal fortune and from the largesse of his "friends," among whom he counted the Las Vegas casino bosses.

When on a quest for donations, he always wore his priestly garb. After he'd concluded his duties as a fundraiser — almost always successfully — he'd loosen his clerical collar and appear in the casino wearing a business suit with a conservative necktie. These were what he called his "recreational breaks," when he would tap a bit more of his personal fortune and try to tempt Lady Luck. The padre was a crapshooter.

He remained in town for a week at a time, visiting various hotel-casinos, humbly accepting donations by day and bellying up to the crap table by night, winning or losing thousands of dollars at a session.

A few weeks after one of his trips, several casinos were paid a visit by a pair of FBI agents who were searching for a phony priest. It seems this man's scam was raising funds for a Church-supported school in the Bay Area; he worked the west coast with the same story, the same costume, and the same brochures and pictures. He'd wormed his way into some of the most exclusive country clubs and had raised literally millions of dollars from corporate leaders with whom he played golf. He was an honorary member of many social organizations and various service clubs. At least the casino bosses weren't alone in being bilked.

The FBI was called in by officials of the Catholic Church after they got wind of what was going on. While the authorities were ready to mount an all-out manhunt for the con man who'd stolen in the name of the Church, the religious leaders believed that the less publicity on this embarrassing situation the better. So, if a distinguished gentleman knocks on your door seeking a donation for a children's camp and brandishes pious photos, beware.

The Banker

For some reason, the San Francisco area produced more than its fair share of memorable individuals who made their marks on Las Vegas. A fitting partner to the phony priest and the million-dollar bettor was the banker. He was the bona fide owner of a medium-sized bank in downtown San Francisco. He, too, was a crapshooter.

Always dressed to the nines in a business suit, vest, and necktie, he carried a walking stick and was an imposing figure as he strutted through the Flamingo Hotel casino.

His demeanor never changed, whether winning or losing. But he was happiest when his bets were being paid with stacks of $100 chips. He didn't use higher-denomination chips because he didn't want to call attention to himself. But he did a pretty good job of that by stacking up those black chips all over the layout. He could easily win or lose $50,000 to $100,000 in a single session, break for lunch, then come back and win or lose another 50 or 100 G's.

The dealers and casino floormen enjoyed his sessions immensely, because he was liberal with tokes. Then one day, officials from the IRS visited the Flamingo to ask questions about the banker and his gambling habits. They were followed by the FBI, the SEC, and California bank examiners. The man's bank had gone broke, with most of the funds lost on the dice tables at the Flamingo.

This turned out to be a big loser for all involved. The banker went to prison. Depositors had to struggle to get their money. And the Flamingo was left holding a worthless marker for more than $300,000. The worst part for the casino was that the banker had used more than $50,000 of the marker to toke casino employees.

Tallulah Wanted Baccarat

Baccarat is a card game of Italian descent, in which the object is to reach a point total of nine, or as close to nine as possible. The odds on baccarat are almost even, with the house holding a little more than a one percent advantage. Because of the five- and six-figure maximum-bet limits and the simplicity of the game, high-stakes players, primarily from the Orient, have adopted baccarat as their game of choice. The complexity of craps has kept it a mystery to Asian players, but baccarat can be learned in a matter of minutes.

Baccarat and its direct ancestor chemin de fer were unknown in Las Vegas until 1953, when a Broadway actress made her nightclub debut at the Sands Hotel shortly after it opened. A world traveler and gambler who'd fallen in love with baccarat in European casinos, Tallulah Bankhead was upset when she couldn't find the game offered anywhere in Las Vegas.

Between and after her shows at the Sands, she'd usually walk next door to Luigi's Restaurant to relax. There was only one problem: Luigi's had no casino. Tallulah continuously badgered Luigi to open a few tables at which she could play—especially a baccarat table.

When Talullah was angry, the world knew about it. Her voice could best be described as a loud rusty foghorn. Luigi and his family finally determined that it would be easier to bring in the game and go into the gambling business than to offend the first lady of Broadway and her many friends, who had also become excellent customers. Back then, about all it took to get a gaming license was filling out some forms and presenting a couple of people in town who would vouch for your honesty.

Thus, when Talullah returned for her repeat appearance at the Sands later in the year, a baccarat table had been installed in Luigi's lounge area. True to her word, Talullah played there, at very high stakes, every night. Her fans and admirers took to the game as well.

One of Bankhead's closest friends was actress Marlene Dietrich, who lived in Beverly Hills and came to Las Vegas during Bankhead's appearances. (She eventually signed her own contract to headline in the resort showrooms.) Dietrich, too, was a baccarat player. Both women were at the height of their fame and Luigi's suddenly became the favorite watering hole for many high rollers, who enjoyed being in the company of the two famous actresses.

The Sands, whose bosses were always alert for an emerging high-roller trend, opened its own baccarat table. As operators of the first casino to deal the game, the bosses forever patted themselves on the back for "discovering" it.

Today baccarat is a fixture in most Strip casinos and still attracts the highest rollers in Nevada. The tragedy is that Tallulah died before baccarat became commonplace on the Strip.

The Old-Time High Rollers

Very few big-time gamblers play as feverishly as Nick the Greek, but a select fraternity of gamblers play as high as the Greek did. In fact, the real magic in Las Vegas and all other gambling jurisdictions is embodied by the "high roller." It's been estimated that there are roughly 5,000 bona fide high rollers in the world, almost all of them men with countless liquid assets who can afford to bet a minimum of $1,000 a hand at the games of their choice.

The profile of the high roller has changed considerably over the years. The original high rollers in my era were the distillers and smugglers of illegal liquor during Prohibition. They had tons of cash and were a flashy set. They enjoyed being in the casinos, which they either owned pieces of or supplied all the illegal hootch for. These were truly two-fisted players. Almost all played for cash only. They'd accept no chips or checks from anyone, even their partners.

Then came World War II, which produced even more high rollers than heroes. Millions of servicemen learned to gamble during the long days and nights spent in their barracks, on the decks of ships, or in the field waiting for their next move. A handful of sharpies got rich off the rubes. The war also made millionaires out of the black marketeers, who never risked anything during the war, but wound up overloaded with illegal earnings never reported to Uncle Sam. The play of the black marketeteers was obscene. They had so much cash, money had little meaning to them.

Then there were the veterans who made their fortunes in the post-war prosperity as entrepreneurs, manufacturers, executives, investors, and professionals in any number of other profitable careers. They were now lifetime gamblers, playing high-stakes games all over the world.

Some awfully strange birds found their way into the Flamingo casino in those days. Many were wannabe high rollers, but some proved to be legitimate. One I always found both strange and legitimate was "Mr. S." This short, plump, plain guy held patents to hundreds of products he'd developed for the war effort, then marketed with a vengeance to consumers after the war. Mr. S. possessed untold millions and, from what we learned, was as quiet and conservative a businessman in his native Chicago as he was wild and outrageous in his adopted Las Vegas.

He showed up at the Flamingo a half-dozen times a year, dressed in an ill-fitting ten-gallon hat, plaid shirt, Levi's, and a pair of hand-crafted cowboy boots. Though he dressed the part, there was never a chance anyone would mistake him for a cowboy. He'd usually bring along a handful of friends, associates, or employees—all comped.

Mr. S. was strictly a crapshooter, and his style drove the dealers nuts. Before coming into the dice pit, he'd usually stop at a change booth and buy six or eight rolls of dimes. Once at the table, which was usually a private game reserved for him and his crew, he'd ask for several thousand dollars in $5 chips for himself, plus $100 in $5 chips for each of his friends. Mr. S. would proceed to drive dealers crazy betting the $5 chips, even when he had a thousand dollars riding on a single roll. When the dice started to fall his way, he always insisted on collecting his payoffs in $5 chips. He'd fill the chip rack in no time, then start shoveling the chips into his ten-gallon hat. The big problem occurred after he'd gone through all the nickel chips in the rack and needed the chips in his hat. He'd dump all those chips onto the layout for the dealer to count out the correct amount for his new bets.

What the casino workers hated most, however, were those coins he'd sometimes use to "liven up" a game. If a winning point was thrown, he'd unwrap a roll of coins and throw them all over the table. Why? To celebrate, for one, but mostly to show he could get away with the prank. The dealers had to go through the long process of lifting each coin off the felt layout.

But they humored him—with good reason. Mr. S. was generally good for a loss approaching a half-million dollars per weekend. More important, he always paid off his markers with a check prior to leaving Las Vegas.

One high roller came as a complete surpise. This was a man highly respected for his business acumen, though he was never thought of as a player, let alone a big player. One afternoon he walked into a major casino and bellied up to a crap table. Quietly and unobtrusively, he began making sizable bets, peeling hundred dollar bills off of a large wad stashed in his jacket pocket.

The man showed little emotion as his bankroll rose and fell. After several hours of play, he had moved quite a bit ahead of the house. At that point he took a break and walked into the coffee shop for dinner. He paid the check and returned to the same table where his winning streak continued.

The businessman played through the night. When the first rays of the morning sun began peeking through the front doors of the casino, he asked a pit boss if he could get a room. Arrangements were made and he adjourned for a few hours of sleep.

While he slept, the dealers chatted among themselves.

One dealer brought up the fact that the high roller hadn't forked over a single gratuity, nor had made a single bet for any of the dealers. The dealers were actually more surprised than upset; most professional casino dealers know that the tokes will be there at the end of a shift and tend not to worry too much about them during play.

The player returned about mid-afternoon and headed directly for the same crap table. He greeted the dealers with whom he had worked the previous day. He launched back into action. Luck still appeared to be with him. He continued to increase his bets. He again played until sunrise, and this time was provided with a suite by the house. He was ahead more than a million dollars.

That afternoon he returned to the casino and again ambled over to the same crap game. He looked around the table to find the same crew that had worked there the previous two afternoons. He turned to the pit boss and asked if the night crew would be the same as the past two nights. The boss checked the schedule and informed the big player that two of the dealers on the night shift were off. The player asked the pit boss to contact the two dealers and ask them to come in for a short time, even though it was their night off. He then left the casino without making a single bet.

Now the casino staff was truly puzzled. An hour later the man was back, carrying a briefcase that appeared to be stuffed with paperwork. He walked past the casino and into the executive offices, emerging a few minutes later with the casino manager. Both appeared happy.

The two men walked to another office, where the casino manager left the high roller while he went to speak to the pit boss. First the pit boss, then the dealers from both shifts—each spent a few minutes in the office.

By the time the high roller left the hotel that evening, he'd taken orders for 16 brand-new cars, which were delivered to all of the dealers and bosses with whom he had dealt — free of charge.

The Modern High Rollers

The post-war rich were more than willing to show off their wealth. The 1950s and '60s turned out more exhibitionist high rollers than the gambling hells in Renaissance England, where so many noblemen and women lost their fortunes.

As the post-war exhibitionist high rollers began to peter out, some very big Latin money began pouring in from Mexico and Central and South America. These gamblers were difficult to categorize. They seemed to range from men who owned big business or large estates with vast reserves of natural resources, to crooked politicians with pipelines that flowed cash into their coffers, to drug czars who brought millions of dollars in international currency that could be effectively laundered in the casinos.

Money laundering became a big business for a few casino operators. They'd allow the traffickers to unload bundles of foreign currency collected from drug buyers in the casino cages in exchange for markers with which to buy chips at the tables. The traffickers would gamble for a while, then cash out the remaining chips for Uncle's greenbacks. The drug dealers, the casinos, and the moneychangers were happy with the arrangement. Not so the Internal Revenue Service. Once IRS agents figured out what was going down, it didn't take them long to shut down the business and track down the malefactors, sending some to federal facilities where they could busy themselves with real laundry.

The brand of high roller that made Las Vegas the lush

opulent resort area of the '50s, '60s, and '70s is no more. Those who weren't lost to attrition were chased away by stringent IRS rules and regulations that nipped at the heels of the big players until they were hobbled.

As the old-style high rollers began to fade away, the new corporate owners of the Las Vegas resorts started scouring the world, looking for replacement players. They pretty well gave up on Mexico after a major devaluation of the peso wiped out many wealthy players.

The European fat cats have literally dozens of countries in their midst that offer every form of gaming imaginable. For them, a trip to Monte Carlo, Switzerland, or England is much more convenient.

The casino moguls finally turned to the Pacific Rim for their next generation of high rollers. Players from Japan, China, Hong Kong, Malaysia, and other Asian countries suddenly found themselves being courted by endless lines of American "hosts," who offered every inducement imaginable to try their luck at a given Las Vegas casino. They could play up to hundreds of thousands of dollars a hand on baccarat, a game by now known equally well in the Western and Eastern worlds. For whatever reason, the Las Vegas salesmen decided they would differentiate between the old high rollers and the new breed by referring to the new big players as "whales." Just what connotation was intended is still beyond me, but so is some of the treatment now being accorded these big fish.

All any well-to-do player in, say, Hong Kong has to do is call his "fairy godfather" in Las Vegas. A limousine will be sent to his home to take him and whomever he wants to bring along to the airport. A chartered jet will fly them all to Las Vegas, where one or more limos will await the whale at the airport. He'll be whisked to the hotel, and a trail of toadies will follow him to a suite at least twice the size of two large homes.

During his stay, the whale and his entourage are put up in 10,000-square-foot penthouse suites complete with swimming pools, butlers, private chefs, and every other amenity imaginable. No city on Earth can entertain moneyed men and women in the style that Las Vegas has perfected.

In return for all of this, the whale knows what he's expected to do: make wagers the size of an average person's mortgage. If he doesn't, he won't be invited back. And even on this trip, if his play is not up to standards, someone will have a fatherly chat with him and, if necessary, he will be asked to go home early — on a commercial jet.

If the whale lives up to what's expected of him, it's likely there will be a substantial change in his bank account — in one direction or another — by the time he wings his way home. There will be a corresponding swing for the casino. It has now gotten to the point where stocks in gambling companies might move up or down by two or three points based strictly on the outcome of a visit by one of these whales.

The biggest casinos now have large staffs out trolling the waters of the world, trying to land a whale or two. Some have marketing offices in the great international cities and can dispatch a company jet to almost any place in the world at a moment's notice.

Casino hosts, who are charged with attracting this type of player to their joints, command salaries and benefits running into seven figures a year. I've even heard of hosts with contracts that pay them a percentage of the losses incurred by their customers. Ironically, the procedures used by the big houses of today to lure the whales are similar to those applied by Chester Simms, Jake Freidman, and other bosses of yesteryear: In a nutshell, they highly personalize the process. The whales' eating, sleeping, drinking, gambling, and even mating habits are known and catered to by the casinos.

But this kind of high roller is the exception to the rule — a tiny fraction of the tens of millions of visitors who come to town, play a little for fun, receive a few perks via electronic tracking systems at the machines, and go home. It's number-crunching, a quick-turnover game, a massive volume play.

Las Vegas used to be about high rollers. These days, it's about high roller coasters.

9

The Bosses

He Helped Write the Book

Chester Simms, the Flamingo casino manager during my tenure there, was a bear of a man who had a permanent scowl across what otherwise would have been a handsome face. He was a long-time veteran of the gaming business, Meyer Lansky's favorite casino boss when Lansky controlled the gambling in Cuba and the Dominican Republic. Simms helped write the book on casino management.

Chester was already at the Flamingo when the casino-hotel was sold to Morris Lansburgh and his partners. It's said that Simms was angry with the Flamingo's real boss (also Lansky) for bringing in someone like Lansburgh who had no gambling experience. "I don't need any numbers guy looking over my shoulder," he was heard saying. "He's just gonna be another bean counter who has no idea what's going on."

Simms had good reason for concern. Lansburgh had been running his Florida resorts successfully for a long time and was used to looking at a daily report of revenues and expenses to determine the hotels' exact rates of profit. But this couldn't be done in a casino.

In the gambling business, the profits are virtually guaranteed by the immutable laws of probability. But though the casino's expected return holds true over the long run, the wins and losses fluctuate enormously from day to day. The handle one day might be quite high, but the place would show a loss. The next day, with the same amount of action, there would be a huge profit. Simms doubted that Lansburgh would know how to interpret the daily figures.

Shortly after taking over management of the Flamingo, Lansburgh told Simms that he wanted to be informed any time a casino customer had a sizable win. Simms grumbled something and went about his business.

A couple of nights later, at four in the morning, the phone rang in Lansburgh's suite at the hotel, awakening him from a sound sleep. "Morris, this is Chester," Simms verily trilled. "Just wanted to let you know we just had a guy come in and hit a $100 jackpot on one of the slot machines. You wanted to know about winners, so I'm keeping you informed." Someone who was there swore that a rare smile crossed Simms' face as he hung up the phone.

The next day Lansburgh sought out Simms, finding him on a massage table at the Flamingo's health club. "Okay, Chester," Lansburgh groused. "You run the damned casino and I'll try to keep my nose out of it."

The two men never argued about their different styles of doing business after that, primarily because both were very successful. However, they would periodically have "discussions," in which Simms would try to explain the casino business to Lansburgh. One day Lansburgh presented what he thought was a logical explanation of how profits are made in business.

"I have an item on the menu in the coffee shop," the

veteran hotelman began. "It's listed at a price that will cover the cost of product, service, and overhead, plus a profit of thirty-three percent. That means that I'll make thirty-three percent every time the item is sold. That figure won't change until either our costs for food, service, or overhead rise, or we decide we want to change our rate of profit. Why can't the same formula hold true for gambling?" he inquired of Simms.

"It does work basically the same way, Morris," the casino manager growled. "However, the expenses we have in taking a dollar from the customer amounts to about a dime, which is primarily a portion of a dealer's salary and floor space. So, we keep about ninety cents out of every dollar that's lost in a casino, while you keep thirty-three cents out of the dollar whenever you serve a meal. Who's in the right business?"

Simms' philosophy of gambling was simple and profound. "Gambling is the most personalized business there is," he would explain. "You're taking money from the gambler without giving him any product or service in return. So you'd better be ready to at least give him a kiss."

It's just as well that Chester and most of his colleagues dating back to the days of illegal casinos either retired or died before the public corporations took over the reins of legalized gaming throughout the country. The old-timers could not have adjusted to the corporate style of "tracking" the casino play of an individual to determine whether he has "earned" a comped room, meal, room service or, perhaps, airfare. In Simms' day, it was up to the casino bosses to determine the actual value of a player, without having to check a computer and get approval for their decisions *from an accountant*.

One of those colleagues showed his true colors shortly after a public corporation had purchased the hotel where he worked. A man who had been a "solid-gold" customer at the casino for years was in town staying at the hotel with an entourage of friends and associates, taking up more than a half-dozen suites. The new general manager called the casino boss into his office and wanted to know why the complimentary accommodations had been extended to the entire group. The casino man explained that the player was an exhibitionist and always brought along a bunch of people whom he financed to shoot craps at a table he would take over for his own play. While he was at it, the casino boss also explained to the new company man that he intended to book the entire group into the hotel's dinner show that evening—on a complimentary basis, of course.

As the casino boss was talking, the general manager was typing away on his computer keyboard. The executive then swung back with a wry smile on his face. "Your big-deal customer hasn't been here for almost a year, and when he left he was stuck for all of two grand. That's worth all those rooms and a dinner show on top of it? Bullshit. That's the kind of freeloader we're getting out of here. You guys better learn how business is really done."

The casino boss didn't say a word. He left the corporate offices and returned to his own office next to the casino cashier's cage. He picked up the phone and placed a call to a buddy at another Las Vegas resort, where the corporate management teams hadn't begun performing their surgery yet. "Ryan, how would you like a new customer?" he asked.

"Always interested," came the response. "What's happening?"

The casino boss identified the customer, who was coveted by every casino in Las Vegas. This player, who owned a large company, was known to have lost millions of dollars over the years, mostly at the casino that no longer wanted him. The last visit had been a fluke: He'd become ill just after arriving in Las Vegas and was barely able to play.

But the casino manager didn't feel he had to explain anything to the new know-it-all general manager. Instead, he told the boss of the rival casino to send limousines over to pick up the entire party. He then explained the situation to the customer, who thanked him for handling the matter.

The casino manager walked down to the keno lounge and scribbled on the back of a blank keno ticket: "I resign, effective immediately." He then went over to the race and sports book and found the raunchiest-looking derelict in the place. He handed him the keno ticket and a $20 bill, instructing him to deliver the note, personally, to the general manager. He then handed the derelict another ten and said that was for spitting on the floor after handing over the note.

That was how the casino old-timers, especially those like Chester Simms, felt about the "bean counters" and "Hahvid MBAs."

Simms saw and understood everything there was to see and understand within a casino; he was also the most observant business executive I've ever known. Many in the gambling business would be amazed when they discovered that Simms had hired another dealer, floorman, or pit boss who'd been fired as a suspected cheat or thief by another casino boss.

Chester's response was to the point: "At least when I hire a cheat, I know he's a cheat and I know how he does it. If I hire someone who hasn't been branded, I've got to learn his scam. But the cheater already knows I know his game and he'll rarely try to use it on me."

The Chester Simms' pronouncement that had the greatest impact on me was one that few people who lived in Las Vegas then (or live here now) would readily admit:

"Las Vegas is really Devil's Island — with privileges. We're three hundred miles from anywhere. We watch people come and go every day. After they're gone, we're still here.

"This town gets down deep into everyone who has ever lived here. Where else can you get a haircut at midnight? Or go grocery shopping at three in the morning? In what other town can you meet friends and sit around and shoot the breeze and watch the sun come up — every night?

"There are no releases from this Devil's Island, only paroles. And almost everyone ever paroled violates that parole and is back here. If you think I'm wrong, leave town. Then see how quickly you return."

It was certainly true in my life.

They Were Professionals

Two casino bosses who played a large part in Las Vegas' development into a first-class resort destination were Sid Wyman and Carl Cohen. Both stood about six feet tall and weighed well over 300 pounds. They were two of the sharpest gambling operators ever to hit the casino industry.

Carl Cohen had been in the illegal casino business until he arrived in Las Vegas and became casino manager for Beldon Katleman, sole owner of the El Rancho Vegas. Cohen's toughest job was getting along with the bombastic Katleman and dealing with his mercurial moods. Cohen finally got tired of working for his boss, left the El Rancho, and took over the casino at the Sands.

During his many years at the Sands, Cohen gained a reputation as one of the most knowledgeable casino bosses in Las Vegas and as one of the nicest men ever to trod the local turf. He and his wife lived in a suite at the Sands, raised a fine family, and were active in all the right causes.

Cohen never made excuses about his obesity. "I love to eat," was all he'd say. He'd always top off a huge meal of appetizer, soup, salad, meat, potatoes, and vegetables with fried bananas. Those calorie-laden, cholesterol-loaded fried bananas were his — and his pal Sid Wyman's — favorite gastronomical delight.

Cohen was well-known throughout the gambling fraternity, but he preferred to maintain a low profile. That became impossible for him one night while Frank Sinatra, the hotel's star performer, was appearing in the Copa Room. Sinatra had been gambling, drinking, and making a nuisance of himself after finishing his show. Cohen managed to avoid a confrontation by dispatching various pit bosses and members of the singer's entourage to try to keep him in line. But when all else failed, Cohen finally moved in and, as politely as possible, asked Sinatra to leave the casino. Sinatra stormed off.

Things were just getting back to normal when the crash of glass resonated from one of the rear entrances to the casino. Obviously unhappy with his ouster, Sinatra had returned to the casino aboard an electric cart used by the gardeners and smashed through a glass door.

Cohen rushed to the scene. An argument ensued. Sinatra decided to play the tough guy and took a swing that missed Cohen. Cohen returned a single punch that cold-cocked the vocalist. That was the last time Sinatra was ever invited to play the Sands. He immediately signed a contract with Caesars Palace, but that didn't work out too well, either. Sinatra got into a hassle with casino boss Sandy Waterman, who pulled a gun and threatened to shoot him.

Cohen stayed with the Sands through a brief procession of owners, finally selling his percentage and moving to Kirk Kerkorian's first MGM Grand Hotel, where he remained until his death.

His close friend and associate, Sid Wyman, was the polar opposite of Cohen in most ways. Wyman had fled St. Louis after the Kefauver Crime Committee hearings in 1950. The Tennessee senator had identified Wyman and his partner, Al Moll, as the largest bookmakers in the Midwest, and Wyman wisely decided it would be best to relocate in Las Vegas, where he could ply his chosen profession with impunity. He became a part owner at the Sands, where he and Cohen hit it off instantly — especially when they learned of each other's love for fried bananas.

Where Cohen was a family man whose only connection with gambling was on the house's side of the table, Sid Wyman was a player. His favorite game was poker, but after baccarat was introduced, it wasn't uncommon to see him win or lose a hundred thousand dollars or more in a single session at the big green table.

Wyman stayed at the Sands until he and Al Moll decided to try their hand as owners and operators of their own resort. They built the Royal Nevada Hotel, which was a beautiful resort, with low-rise bungalow buildings surrounding a fabulously lush pool area. It also had a great location, across the Strip from (and a little north of) the Desert Inn. But the Royal Nevada opened at the worst possible time: 1955. That same year the Dunes, Riviera, Hacienda, and Moulin Rouge opened; the Showboat had opened a year earlier out on Boulder Highway and the 15-story Fremont was being built downtown.

In addition, the Tropicana was under construction down the Strip and the Stardust was going up right next door to the Royal Nevada. The building boom wiped out several well-intentioned and well-heeled groups, among them

Wyman and Moll.

The original owners of the Riviera went broke during the same shakeout, and a group of Wyman's friends took over the property. Sid bought into the action and stayed with the Riviera, as the Strip's first high-rise hotel, reaching nine stories, grew into one of the most successful properties in Las Vegas.

Wyman wound up his colorful career as a point holder in the Dunes, gravitating to the high-stakes poker played in the Dunes cardroom. He and partner Major Riddle joined in the action in their own joint, until Nevada's gaming authorities passed a ruling that prohibited owners from playing in their own casinos. Finally Wyman bowed out of Las Vegas and traveled the country, playing in no-limit poker games until the end.

Shooting Craps for an Upper Plate

Chester Simms, Sid Wyman, and Carl Cohen weren't the only eagle-eyed casino employees. All over town, pit bosses had to contend with all sorts of craziness. I'll never forget one New Year's Eve.

Every night in Las Vegas seems like New Year's Eve in the casino, but on the real New Year's Eve, Las Vegas shoots into orbit. In the old days, it was the one night of the year when customers and hotel and casino bosses wore formal attire. Casinos raised their minimum wagers. The majority of the throngs jamming every hotel were high rollers invited as guests of the house. They'd be wined and dined in the best Las Vegas fashion. They reciprocated by snapping the rubber bands off their wads of cash and playing with unusual abandon. It was New Year's Eve, after all (as if there was something different about gambling on the final evening of the year).

The crowd was really into the swing of things at the Dunes that night. When the clock struck twelve, everyone went through the ritual of greeting the New Year. Wives and all the other women in the area were dutifully kissed, horns were blown, and streamers were thrown. Then it was time to get down to business.

A solid mass of humanity tried to get every last nickel into every slot machine and onto every table in the house. One customer elbowed his way to a crap table. The floormen and pit bosses gently moved some of the lower-limit players a few inches each way until there was space for the high roller. The man started right in betting big and his fortune was ever-changing. He couldn't get a real hot streak going, but he was able to hold his own.

At one point, the dice turned in favor of the player and the high roller got right into the swing of it, yelling and cheering and pleading for the dice to remain friendly. He got a little carried away with his yelling and his upper denture plate flew out of his mouth and onto the table. With absolutely no delay, a Dunes pit boss, Sherlocke Feldman, reached into his own mouth, removed his own denture, dropped it onto the table, and yelled, "You're faded!"

Another crap-table goof wasn't considered quite so funny. A previous shooter had sevened out, so the dice were passed to the next shooter—a "mucho macho" dude in a leather pants-and-shirt outfit and draped from neck to wrist with heavy gold jewelry. He was throwing hundred-dollar bills on the table and making it known that he was "the man."

When the tray of dice was passed to him, he made a big display of selecting a pair that met his approval. Then, jangling loudly, he shook the dice violently and dropped them on the table in front of himself several times, as if he were checking to make certain they had all their spots. Finally, the boxman controlling the game exhorted the player to roll the dice. The macho guy finally let them go, along with a roar that could be heard three hotels away. The only problem was that he let go of three dice instead of two, having had one of the cubes stashed in his sleeve. The loaded die he tried to get into the game was supposed to sail out with one of the legitimate dice provided by the casino, while he palmed and pocketed the other one.

As every player looked at the dude, the boxman made a silent signal and two beefy security guards instantly flanked the shooter. Then the boxman looked at the much-subdued macho man and exclaimed, "You rolled a six, a four, and a three, sport. Your number is thirteen. How do you plan to make it with *two* dice?"

The cheater was escorted out by the security guards, then turned over to the cops to face charges of cheating a gaming establishment, a felony in Nevada.

The General Led His Troops Well

Hans Eichenwaller arrived in the United States at the age of 13, unable to speak a word of English. His parents had snuck his sister and him out of their native Germany as the extermination of Jews in Europe was getting under way. He never heard another word from his parents or the rest of the family, all of whom apparently died in the Nazi prison camps.

Hans and his sister were taken in by family members who'd left Germany long before and had settled in Detroit. He was intent on becoming an American and making his adopted country proud of him. First he shook off his lengthy German name and became known as Harry Wald. The next step was to learn English. But immigrant or broken English would never do. If Harry Wald was going to be an American, he would speak as Americans do. So he worked doubly hard to completely shed his accent.

After completing the arduous task of transforming himself into a complete American, Wald stayed in the public school system until he was old enough to join the Army as a buck private. His fierce patriotism, along with his desire to help whip the Nazis, did not go unnoticed. Wald worked his way up through the ranks and ultimately retired as a full colonel.

Nevada's governor at the time was Mike O'Callaghan, a much-decorated Marine Corps veteran of the Korean War. O'Callaghan admired Wald to the extent that he considered Harry a general, whether his collar showed the insignia or not. The governor, never one to be hampered by red tape, petitioned the Department of the Army to have Harry Wald named the head of the Nevada National Guard and insisted that Wald be accorded the one-rank promotion that went with the appointment. That was how Wald became a brigadier general, an honor he cherished for the rest of his life.

Harry had learned well during his days in the military. A stern yet soft-spoken officer, he directed his troops with authority and fairness. He also knew that no matter how high he rose on the ladder, there was always someone a rung higher to whom he would be answerable.

Harry had come to know some of the original investors in Caesars Palace even before plans for the property were completed and the principals wanted him to oversee the building of the fabulous resort. So Harry Wald moved right in with Nate Jacobson and Jay Sarno, the geniuses who'd dreamed up the Caesars concept.

Wald oversaw construction from beginning to end and was named general manager of the entire property, a post he held for more than 20 years under a revolving door of owners. He liked it best when the hotel had a president who was open and outgoing, which allowed Harry to remain behind the scenes, directing the operation.

Harry's routine at Caesars started the same way every day, six days a week. His first stop was the barber shop, where Joey Trujillo, the most popular barber in Las Vegas, held court. Each morning, Joey would shampoo Harry's silver mane and comb it out. Harry Wald always looked like he just stepped out of a full-page ad in a gentlemen's magazine.

Then it was into his office to go over whatever might have occurred since he'd left the property at about two o'clock the same morning. After taking care of correspondence and phone calls, Harry would leave his office and sometimes not return for many hours.

He was into every nook and cranny of "his" hotel. Every employee, supervisor, and executive at the luxury property knew they would be seeing their boss as frequently when things were going well as when there were problems. He knew the vast majority of the thousands of employees by name. Of course, they knew his name, too. However, not many of the staff ever referred to him as Mr. Wald; even fewer addressed him as Harry. He was "The General."

During his years at the helm of the classiest operation in Las Vegas, Wald came to know top gambling executives and players from all parts of the world. In the mid-1970s, when legalized casinos were popping up all over London, English casino owners and operators literally waited in line outside Harry's office for an audience. Also in the '70s, when oil-rich Arabs had to find ways to spend their newfound wealth, it was Harry who flung open the doors of Caesars to entertain them. During this time, Harry turned down huge offers to take over the operation of casinos all over the world.

Inevitably, as with most of the old-time resort executives who labored so long and hard in building their own properties and in turning Las Vegas into the most prominent resort city in the world, Harry Wald became a dinosaur.

He was perfectly capable of operating Caesars and answering to whomever was the majority owner at the time. But he didn't fit into the corporate mold. He was too used to doing things when and how he felt they should be done to start wading through the many layers of corporate management. He became frustrated when the things he'd been doing on a daily basis now had to be submitted to nameless faceless committee members for approval.

Finally Harry Wald was given the boot. He wasn't bitter—until he started seeing the property slipping in prestige. Caesars began to lose its long-held *crème de la crème* reputation. Many of the other top executives bailed out as well.

But what hit Harry the hardest was when the owner of the hotel, the man who'd invited him to leave, came out with the following statement during a newspaper interview: "I'm a businessman. I don't know anything about gambling, other than that it's a business. I don't even go into the casino. I hire people to handle that portion of the business, same as I do all the other parts of our operation."

Reading that statement about his beloved Caesars Palace was like having someone poke a stick into his eyes, and he never really recovered. This strong vital individual literally wasted away.

Several years after he left Caesars, he died during surgery at Walter Reed Army Hospital. But Hans Eichenwaller got his final wish: He was buried in Arlington National Cemetery with full military honors accorded to a general in the U.S. Army.

10

The Owners

Beldon the Maverick

Tom Hull built the El Rancho Vegas in 1941, but he was a little ahead of his time. Only a few years later, management and money difficulties forced Hull to sell the first motor inn-casino on the Strip to Beldon Katleman, a guy who marched strictly to his own drummer. Katleman's family, which made its fortune in real estate throughout the country, handled most of the purchase price of El Rancho Vegas for Beldon. It was rumored that the family wanted to provide him with gainful employment to keep him away from the family businesses.

Katleman was a maverick in every way, shape, and form. A true contrarian, he did everything backward from what seemed reasonable or obvious. You could look out the office window and see that the sun was shining and Beldon would practically convince you it was raining.

As sole owner of one of the town's major properties, Beldon Katleman believed he was entitled to his own set of rules. An example of this occurred when the owners of the major properties banded together and agreed to hold down some of the wildly escalating salaries of star entertainers. The group of owners determined that one way to keep the salaries at a workable level was for hotels to stop raiding each other's stars, a practice that drove costs sky-high.

Katleman, who'd never been known as a talent raider, cast his vote in favor of both policies. Meeting adjourned. But the whole confab seemed to give him the idea. Two days later, he approached Joe E. Lewis, who was appearing at the El Rancho Vegas' across-the-Strip neighbor, the Sahara, and offered to double his salary. The move scuttled the entire plan. Salaries continued skyrocketing.

While he owned El Rancho Vegas, Katleman also held 25 percent of the stock in the Last Frontier, his other next-door neighbor, though a mile down the Strip. A group that owned the famed Chez Paris Nightclub in Chicago was interested in purchasing the Frontier, but wanted total control. The owners stood to cash out with tremendous profits if the deal was done, and they pleaded with Katleman to sell. But Beldon wouldn't budge, even under intense heat from his partners.

One of the Chicago group's tactics was to approach me. The investors had heard I was one of the few people Katleman seemed comfortable around. They offered me two percent of the stock in the Last Frontier if I could convince Katleman to sell. Knowing Beldon, I never mentioned the deal I'd been offered. But I did ask periodically if he had changed his mind.

One night I happened to be in the El Rancho chuck-wagon at about 1 a.m. Katleman, sitting at a table across the room, beckoned me to join him. He'd somehow come to know the entire arrangement I'd worked out with the Chicago people, and said that he was thinking of selling.

I was immediately suspicious and grilled him at length

about his motives. With utter sincerity, he made it clear that he wanted to sell and to do so through me. Sugarplum casino points danced through my head.

Then he asked, "Do they still want the Last Frontier?"

"Do they want it? One of the principals called just a couple days ago, asking if there'd been any progress."

Beldon smiled. "Get them right out to Las Vegas. Let's make this deal."

Needless to say, I spent the next 24 hours flying in people from Chicago. I talked to Katleman once. I was the only one he would speak to, and yes, he told me, the deal was on. But then we had to wait till the next day for one of the group to arrive from Paris. Finally we all piled into my Plymouth for the ride to the El Rancho, where I pulled up in front of Katleman's personal cottage.

After a few moments, he came to the door, still wearing his robe and looking like he'd just awakened, though it was one o'clock in the afternoon. After a few nodded introductions and no offers of a handshake, Katleman asked what we were doing there. I protested vociferously. He looked me square in the eye and said, "Yeah, I was interested in selling the hotel. But that was over twenty-four hours ago. Deal's off." And that was that.

Another deal I saw go south involved the owners of the Thunderbird Hotel (now the wretched hulk of the El Rancho—not the original one, but the old Thunderbird, which changed its name to the Silverbird, then El Rancho, then closed in 1992). The Thunderbird group wanted to open a horseracing track behind their place. Because of the size of the plot, the track would extend 30 feet onto land owned by Katleman—a fairly small vacant parcel between the Thunderbird and the Sahara. About the only time anyone noticed the piece of land was when a summertime gullywasher would come ripping across the Strip from Ted

Griss's acreage and wash out the little lot.

Katleman was all "sures" and "of courses" when dealing with his colleagues from across the Strip. He "liked their idea of introducing horseracing to Las Vegas" and he "wanted to help them all he could. Why certainly they could extend the track onto his property," and he "wouldn't even think of charging them any rent." The track opened — this was around 1957, as I recall — and was a moderate success for a few months. Then one morning, the Thunderbird owners received a letter from Katleman's attorney informing them that they were to remove their racetrack from his land. He was just being a jerk, as usual.

In 1960, El Rancho Vegas burned to the ground, in what fire officials called "obvious arson" (no one was ever arrested as a suspect in the torching). It was impossible to find even one damp eye in town when people heard about the blaze: Everyone in Las Vegas knew of Katleman's lack of respect for the town that had made him a very rich man. Following the fire, there was some talk about the maverick rebuilding. But there was also talk that a group of hotel owners invited him to leave town — one of those offers he couldn't refuse. He resettled in Beverly Hills.

Katleman eventually sold the El Rancho tract to another maverick who played by his own rules: Howard Hughes. But he refused to part with the small parcel across the Strip between the Thunderbird and Sahara. Milton Prell, the respected owner of the Sahara who was in the process of buying the already-fading Thunderbird, tried one last time to deal with the mercurial Katleman. Prell showed him plans for a shopping and recreational facility between the two properties, which would effectively turn them into a single entity. Katleman, of course, would hear none of it.

To this day, many old-timers feel that Katleman's refusal to allow Prell's development plan doomed the north end of the Strip. Nearly 40 years later, the old El Rancho Vegas property is still vacant. The new El Rancho (neé Thunderbird) is the only shuttered joint on the Strip, and has been since 1992. Katleman's oddball piece of property is now the home of Wet 'n Wild, the big water park next to the Sahara. Bill Bennett left Circus Circus and bought the Sahara. He's busy bucking the tide, trying to breathe some life back into what was once the busiest intersection in Las Vegas.

Two-Fisted Five-Foot Gambler

Jake Freidman was a point holder in and the president of the Sands Hotel when it opened in 1952. This diminutive Jewish cowboy from Texas, who spoke with a distinctive Eastern European accent and reeked of White Shoulders perfume, was one of the truest characters ever to hit the Las Vegas gambling scene. His friendly and flamboyant personality perfectly symbolized the town during its formative years.

Jake Freidman had been involved with rum-running during Prohibition. He'd also been a boss gambler when and where it was illegal, so he could, I suppose, be considered a mobster. But while many of his partners in victimless crime kept their faces hidden and wanted no part of the limelight, Freidman was a showman. And the Sands, in its early years, was showbiz central for Las Vegas and the country.

Freidman stood barely five feet tall, though when he was attired in one of his many distinctive cowboy outfits, with the boots and big Stetson, he appeared quite a bit taller. He did ride horses and I always wondered whether he commanded them in English or Yiddish.

His wearing of White Shoulders perfume was a curios-
ity. Freidman was as far from effeminate as a man could
be, yet he liked to drench himself in the same perfume
women so carefully touched behind their ears and on their
wrists. One night, a female tourist walked up to him and
asked if he was wearing White Shoulders, one of the most
popular scents of the day. Freidman fixed her with a flinty
stare and said, "Yep," then turned away. It was understood
that no one was ever to ask him, "Why the White Shoulders?"

Freidman was one of the premier crapshooters of the
day and he insisted on playing for cash. He wanted no part
of chips. He carried a wad of hundred-dollar bills, he bet
them by the handful, and he wanted to be paid the same
way. A hundred thousand dollars was not an unusual bankroll for Freidman to carry for a couple of hours of dice-shooting.

Freidman couldn't walk past a crap table, even in his
own joint. His action at the Sands didn't sit well with the
state regulators, who feared collusion. So he played around.
He moved through Las Vegas like a whirlwind. When he
and his entourage of pretty girls and hangers-on invaded a
casino, the temperature would immediately rise. Some casinos found it necessary to send a "bag man" to buy up
hundred-dollar bills from a competitor so they'd have
enough to pay off Freidman if he won big. On a couple of
occasions, casino managers contacted bank managers and
had them race to their offices, no matter the hour, to get a
supply of "C" notes.

Freidman was never boisterous at a table, nor was he
an exhibitionist when playing—aside from his fetishes for
hundreds, White Shoulders, and outlandish cowboy attire.
However, he did attract too much attention from the gam-

ing authorities, who finally ruled against an owner playing in his own casino and ordered that regular chips be used for gambling. No more stacks of hundred-dollar bills.

While it may have made things easier for the regulators, accountants, and dealers, these edicts stripped away a little of the fun that was Las Vegas. When Jake Freidman could no longer throw down a hundred $100 bills to make a bet on a crap table, and when Sid Wyman could no longer sit in on the high-stakes games at his own Dunes, a certain measure of excitement left the casinos forever. (Well, not exactly forever: the regulation against "money plays" was rescinded in 1984, but it had long since done its damage.)

He Was Bigger Than Texas

Benny Binion was tough. No one really knew whether he was quite as tough as the legends claimed. But he always carried a small pistol inside one of his custom-made cowboy boots, and stories have it that Benny racked up at least a dozen notches in his revolver handle even before leaving his native Texas in the late 1940s to spend the rest of his life in Las Vegas' legalized gambling business.

As casino operators go, Binion was a gambler. The legends about Benny in the casino far surpassed those about him as a man who was ready and able to protect his position by whatever means necessary. He was known far and wide as the fairest gambling boss around, and he would handle bets so big they might match the total value of his casino. He had no fear.

It was during Benny's salad days as a Texas boss gambler that the organized crime families noticed this grisled Texan, who admitted to just three years of formal education. When they took a closer look at the business he was doing and calculated his profits, they decided they wanted what they considered to be their share.

Binion, of course, didn't agree, especially when they tried to strong-arm him into it.

The boys would head for Texas in their pinstriped suits, perfectly blocked fedoras, black patent-leather shoes, and fancy sunglasses. Most of them went home battered and bruised. According to some reports, a few went home in boxes.

As more and more crime families tried and failed to cut themselves a piece of Binion's action, his reputation as a tough guy quickly grew. Finally Meyer Lansky himself decided to meet this apparently invincible young man. As the accountant and banker for the East Coast mob, Lansky never resorted to strong-arm tactics — personally. But it was said that some of those who had tried to "talk some sense into" Binion had been sent by him.

Lansky made certain his visit to Texas was well-announced. He wanted no part of a possible ambush by this man Binion, whose reputation had grown into a cross between Paul Bunyan and the Dalton Gang all rolled into one mean Texan. According to Binion, the meeting was cordial and the two men parted with total respect for one another. Separate conversations with each man confirm this. (I was told Lansky's side of the story by the author of the book, *Lansky*.) Binion made it clear that he was an independent operator. Lansky agreed it should stay that way.

At the same time, Lansky, whose word had become the underworld's law in Las Vegas, invited Binion to join the action in the emerging southern Nevada market. And eventually, when the heat became unbearable in Texas, Benny took Meyer up on his invitation and moved to cool Las Vegas, where he opened his Horseshoe Casino, in the heart of downtown. Under the careful guidance of Benny, his wife Teddy Jane, and their children, the Horseshoe became the most successful casino in all of Las Vegas.

From the time he first opened in Las Vegas, Binion made it known that a gambler's first wager would establish the maximum bet he could lay. The normal Las Vegas house limit in those days was $500 per bet, which could be made by anyone at any time. Some casinos, though, reduced their risk by maintaining a $200 limit.

But if you wanted to gamble with higher limits at the Horseshoe, you made it known by wagering your chosen amount as your first play. If you laid $1,000 on the table, that would signify your limit for that session of play. If your initial bet was $10,000, Binion would handle your action up to the ten grand. And so far as I know, Benny Binion was the only casino operator ever to accept single bets of a million dollars on a table game.

Naturally, Binion wound up with the highest of the high rollers. Players who hit their heads on the limits at the other casinos in town would gravitate to the Horseshoe, where they could stand as tall as they liked. Benny would send a limousine to deliver them downtown.

Benny brought up his oldest son, Jack, to take over the Horseshoe, and Jack knows the gaming business as well as anyone alive. He ought to—he learned the hard way and still carries a few scars from the school he attended. Benny was always proud to regale listeners with tales of how he trained his eldest. He told a story about one visit to the family's Montana ranch when Jack was about 10 years old.

It seems that father and son left the ranch house early one summer morning to ride out and check fences. Benny could never be bothered with Jeeps or pickup trucks on the ranch. He much preferred the saddle and the open air. So Jack had already become a sound rider. According to Benny, they rode several miles, with Jack pausing now and again to drink some water from his canteen. Benny warned Jack to save some water for later. But even before the sun was directly overhead, Jack had emptied his canteen. Benny paid him no attention, until a thirsty Jack stopped his horse and demanded that his father hand over his canteen.

Benny ordered Jack to dismount. Once the boy was on the ground, Benny gave him a choice. He could either stop his whining, get back on his horse, and wait until they reached a water hole, or he could have his dad's canteen and walk back to the ranch house. As would be natural for a 10-year-old, Jack opted for the immediate drink. But then he had to survive the long arduous trek back to the house. "That boy sure learned a great lesson," Benny proudly proclaimed.

I became friendly with Benny Binion much later in my Las Vegas days, after I'd resurrected my journalism career and was writing a column on happenings within the gaming industry for the short-lived *Valley Times*. I decided to do a column on him, even though we'd met in passing only a few times. The day the column appeared, I received a phone call from Jack Binion. "My pa wants to see you," was the terse message.

This reminded me of the time Gus Greenbaum had wanted to see me a few decades earlier and I began to worry whether I might have gotten some of my facts incorrect in the column. After all, I wrote it without even attempting to speak with Benny; I simply tried to put together a few anecdotes that were common knowledge in Las Vegas.

I went to the Horseshoe and tried to find Benny's office. But Benny didn't have an office — the whole casino was his office. I was told he was probably in the coffee shop, where I found him sitting with his son. Jack waved to me. I went to the table, where I was ordered to be seated. Benny was enjoying what I later learned was one of his favorite meals: Texas chili. At the Horseshoe, the chili was made with the hottest chili peppers imaginable and was always served with about a half-inch of grease atop the bowl. The grease was supposed to soothe some of the heat from the peppers.

"Where'd you ever get all that stuff you wrote about me? I never even talked to you, did I?" Binion got right to the point.

"No sir," I replied. "I think this is the first time we've ever really formally met. But the information I had in the column was pretty much a composite of the Benny Binion known to the average Las Vegan. If I happened to have anything in there that was incorrect, I apologize and will correct it—"

He cut me off in mid-sentence. "No, no, there's nothing wrong. I just wondered how you could get all that stuff without even talking to me. No, everything in there was right. But I'd like to know how you know so much about me?"

I explained that he was an institution in Las Vegas and virtually anything he did was considered news. I also reminded him that during my stint as a cub reporter at the *Las Vegas Sun*, some 20 years earlier, I'd met him when I covered the story about his having to return to Texas and a federal prison on an income-tax charge. That part of his past truly rankled Binion, who felt he was railroaded by some business enemies he had left in the Lone Star State.

Benny and I spent a lot of time together after that meeting. Whenever I had a few hours to spare, I would join him for lunch to be regaled at length with tales of all types. Binion was a born storyteller. It took some study and understanding to separate the wheat from the chaff. According to Benny, there were stories and then there was "graveyard information." When Benny told me something was "graveyard," that meant it was never to be repeated. It meant the information would go to the grave with him, and he expected it to go to the grave with me.

Throughout our relationship, I did everything possible to convince Benny to collaborate with me, or even with another writer, on an autobiography. I was certain, and told him so, that it would be a bestseller. His response was always the same: "No books, no nuthin'. What I know, I know, and it's goin' to the graveyard with me." Even when I tried to get him to agree to prepare a book, but not to release it until after his death, he flatly refused.

When I finally decided to leave the gaming industry, many people in Las Vegas were sure I would write the great exposé on the town, since I had lived there so long and had seen and heard so much private and secret information over the years. However, writing such a book would necessitate violating promises I'd made to too many people, especially Benny Binion and Moe Dalitz. Both men told me "graveyard" stories, which will never be repeated.

(Moe Dalitz rarely spoke to anyone for publication, though he submitted to my interviews on several occasions. But Benny Binion did, finally, talk to Mary Ellen Glass, who put together the definitive oral history on Benny for the University of Nevada Oral History Program, which is available in the Special Collections Department of the UNLV library. Of course, even though the book is more than 100 pages long, Benny didn't tell Ms. Glass much. The interview is a masterpiece of dissembling and vagueness.)

I can, however, repeat information obtained while doing my work, or just being the proverbial fly on the wall. For example, one day I was having lunch with Binion when he received a phone call. He picked up the receiver, listened for a moment, then said, "Hello Meyer. How you feeling?

Won your election, I see." Since it was 1977 and the day after the election approving gambling in Atlantic City, I could only assume that the party on the other end of the line was Meyer Lansky.

The two men spoke for a few minutes and I caught the drift of their conversation. I was getting quite a kick out of it, since New Jersey state officials had been so adamant that the Garden State's gaming industry would have absolutely no underworld participation.

I already knew about Lansky's involvement. During the time I was still at the Flamingo, I learned that Lansky and some of his colleagues had purchased a company called Mary Carter Paints, and the first gaming license to be issued in Atlantic City was to Mary Carter Paints. When Binion got off the phone, he informed me that he had been speaking with "your old boss." He added that Lansky had offered him a casino location and license in Atlantic City. Because of his knowledge of the gaming industry, along with his promotional abilities, Binion was constantly being invited into partnerships of all types. But he respectfully declined Lansky's offer.

Binion was a fabulous promoter. Of all the attractions he developed, the best was his collection of a hundred brand-new $10,000 bills, mounted in a Plexiglas horseshoe near one entrance of the casino. The exhibit has been there since the early 1950s and is the last big-money display (once common around the state) left in Nevada. Visitors pose in front of the million dollars to take home as a free souvenir photograph. I sat with Binion one day as a banker was making it clear that Benny was losing money by keeping the million on display, explaining how much interest he could be earning.

Binion listened politely, then gave this response: "Don't forget the insurance premiums I pay on that million dollars right out in the open. Yeah, I could be making interest on that money, but I'd have to pay taxes on it, wouldn't I? And how about how much it's worth to have millions of people a year walk into my place just to see that million dollars and to have their picture taken alongside that Horseshoe identification? Then tell me what the value is when each of those folks takes their picture home and shows it to their friends. No, Mr. Banker," he concluded, "you go on helping other folks to make lots of money. I'll just keep struggling to keep the doors open."

Binion could speak promotion all he wanted since his official title at the Horseshoe was Director of Public Relations. (According to one source, Benny was never licensed as a casino operator.) One time while I was employed at the Four Queens, across Fremont Street from the Horseshoe, I approached my boss, David Hood, and asked for a raise. He appeared agreeable and inquired about an amount. I suggested that we take an average of the salaries of the other public relations executives in the downtown area and base my raise on that amount.

At the time, there were only three other PR managers—including Binion, whose salary was about a half-million dollars a year. Hood didn't agree with my thinking.

Mrs. Benny Binion, Teddy Jane, was about as frugal as Benny was magnanimous. It was funny to watch the two totally different personalities at work. Benny was a gambler through and through. Instead of regular buttons on his shirts, he wore gold pieces. Teddy Jane was constantly on him to replace them with buttons so the gold could be held in safekeeping. Teddy Jane was the Horseshoe's Chancellor of the Exchequer. She was in complete charge of finances and spent virtually every waking hour working in the casino cashier's office.

One day I was having lunch with Benny and Teddy Jane

when Jack joined us, carrying a set of plans for a new hotel and casino he and the rest of the family wanted to build on land adjacent to the Horseshoe. Benny was still straddling the fence on the idea because, he said, "I won't be around long enough to have to worry about it." He meant that he'd be agreeable if the rest of the family wanted it. But because of his advanced age and illness, it would be up to the family to operate it.

But Teddy Jane, who hated the idea of risking money on anything, was filled with arguments against the plan. Hard as Jack tried to convince his mother of the plan's value, she continued to resist. Finally she said, "Your plans are excellent, Jack. But what happens if there's any kind of a downturn in the economy and we get strapped for cash?"

I had to laugh. Everyone in southern Nevada knew the Binions were one of the wealthiest families in the state and probably had the largest hoard of greenbacks in Nevada as well. But here was Teddy Jane, crying poor as usual.

I couldn't help saying, "If things turn that bad, Mrs. Binion, I guess the only solution will be for you to dig up another can or two of cash from your backyard!"

The Binions built and lived in a large two-story home that was a cross between a ranch house and a fortress. They stayed in that house all the years their family was together. But once the children were all out of the house, Benny and Teddy Jane decided it would be more convenient for them to move into the hotel, which consisted of a few dozen old rooms above the casino. They took two rooms and lived there, quite content.

After Benny's death in 1989, Jack took over the reins of the business. One of his first moves was to purchase the financially troubled Mint Hotel and Casino, a modern highrise next door to the Hoseshoe. He then knocked out a wall and expanded the Horseshoe casino so it was an entire block long. He wanted to situate his mother in one of the beautiful suites atop the Mint portion of the building. But Teddy Jane would have none of that. Those two old rooms in the original Horseshoe were her domain and remained that way until her passing in 1995.

The Horseshoe seemed to be rolling along fine under the direction of Jack Binion. But then his sister Becky Binion Behnen started making noises about filing suit against Jack, claiming he'd used corporate funds to support some new gaming ventures he was starting up in Louisiana.

Finally, in a convoluted financial arrangement, Jack turned over the famed Horseshoe to his sister to operate. Meanwhile, Teddy Binion was forced to sell all of his Horseshoe stock to Becky when his gaming license was revoked by state authorities for drug violations and underworld associations. Shortly after the transaction, Teddy, 55, died of an apparent overdose.

His Money Couldn't Save Him

Howard Hughes was a gambler—when it came to airplanes, oil fields, casinos, or any other of his many penchants. But there is scant evidence that he ever bellied up to a crap table or even dropped a nickel into a slot machine. (Some reports have him shooting dice at the Desert Inn in the 1950s, before he got really weird.)

Hughes loved Las Vegas. The wealthy and eccentric millionaire started frequenting southern Nevada in the early 1950s and settled into a suite at the Flamingo Hotel. Then he took another suite and invited some of his business associates to join him. By the time he finished inviting people to join him for his "short visit" to Las Vegas, he'd taken over an entire wing at the Flamingo.

In those years, Hughes was still somewhat of a man about town. But he was already at the point where he was constantly surrounded by his aides, and some of the eccentricities that blossomed in later years were in their early stages of growth. For example, only hotel employees who'd been personally screened and approved by Hughes were allowed into his wing.

Abe Schiller, the Flamingo's public-relations executive at the time, caught Hughes' eye and became his liaison with the hotel. If Hughes wanted something from the hotel, he passed the word through Schiller. If the hotel wanted to be brought current on payment, Schiller would approach Hughes personally. It was a good relationship.

One incident always stood out in Schiller's memory. Hughes called him to his suite, where Schiller found him in the sitting room holding a large pink blanket, one of the standard linens the Flamingo used on its beds.

"Here, Abe, help me with this," the aeronautical genius instructed. Schiller took one end of the blanket and followed Hughes into the spacious bedroom. While Schiller held the blanket, Hughes came up with a couple of clothespins, with which he hooked the blanket to the curtain rod. Draped over the large picture window, the blanket blocked Hughes' panoramic view of the mountains and desert. Hughes stepped back and admired his work. He then sat on the bed, turned on the lamp, picked up a book, and turned it in various directions to test the light for reading. Finally he gave the makeshift curtain his approval. "That's absolutely perfect, Abe. Now, I want the exact same blankets placed over every window in my rooms."

Schiller wasn't sure he understood what Hughes meant. "You mean, you want the blankets to cover the windows in here, and your sitting room, and the other bedroom?" he asked.

"Yes, and put them up in all the other rooms I've booked, too," Hughes answered. "And make sure you leave the drapes up—put the blankets up over the drapes. But you'd better take this one from my room, so you can be sure to duplicate it exactly. I want every blanket to be the same weight, color, and weave. No variations."

Schiller took the blanket straight to Dick Chappel, the hotel manager and told him that he needed to know the exact number of windows in the Hughes wing. The manager did some quick figuring. Schiller then gave the blanket to the purchasing agent and told him he needed 78 of precisely the same blankets as quickly as possible. He then contacted the chief engineer, told him the blankets would be coming, and gave him instructions on how they were to be mounted, making certain the drapes in the room were untouched.

Once the blankets were delivered and mounted, Schiller heard some grumbling from the Hughes associates, who were unhappy about having their magnificent views impeded. But the boss had called for the ridiculous bedding to be hung over the windows; therefore, so be it. At least there was still a little pinkish daylight filtering through. Except in Hughes' own rooms, where the blackout drapes were kept closed 24 hours of every day. Unless an electric light was turned on, the rooms were in total darkness.

Of course, Hughes never explained why he wanted the blankets in addition to the blackout drapes. Nor would he discuss why the rooms occupied by his staff members had to have the pink blankets. He was in a position where he didn't have to explain anything to anyone.

Hughes attended nightclub shows in various hotels and frequently selected young ladies from the chorus lines to be his "dates." Jimmy Vernon, a former New York club operator then on the Hughes payroll, approached the girls. Seldom did they turn down an invitation from the man who was already famous as one of the richest and most mysterious men in the world.

In many instances, young ladies invited for a date were stood up, because Hughes either forgot about them or decided there was something else he wanted to do. But the select few who met Hughes were picked up in his limousine and spent the evening tagging along with him, attending another show, having coffee or cocktails, or sitting by his side as he discussed business. One thing all of Hughes' dates had in common: Each received a mink coat from him.

Hughes kept himself busy during that first extended Las Vegas stay in the early '50s, which lasted more than a year. He'd earlier gained title to a huge tract of barren desert at the western end of Las Valley Valley. Hughes' dream for this land was to build the world's largest airport, surrounded by all his aircraft and tool plants. The land remained undeveloped until after his death, but in the last 10 years or so, the Hughes Company has developed Summerlin, the largest master-planned community in the country, which bears the name of Hughes' grandmother. On a portion of the property is the magnificent retirement community, Sun City.

Another unknown incident occurred during that same time period. Hughes was forced to appear in a Los Angeles courtroom for a case that has long since been forgotten. The legal aspects were no big deal at the time; the big news was that the notoriously publicity-shy Howard Hughes would be forced to appear in public.

Photographers and TV cameramen followed Hughes from the courtroom to an elevator in the Hall of Records Building, snapping all the photos they could of the man who hated cameras. Two photographers even forced their way into the elevator, only to have themselves physically thrown out by two of Hughes' bodyguards.

A few months after that incident, Hughes' philanthropy overcame his dislike of photographers. One night there was a train wreck along the Union Pacific tracks in one of the most desolate parts of the god-forsaken country near the Nevada-California border. The city editor at the *Los Angeles Mirror* dispatched a photographer to the site in a small private plane to get some first-hand pictures. Strong crosswinds caused the small plane to crash near the scene of the train accident. The pilot was killed; the photographer, badly injured, was taken to Southern Nevada Memorial Hospital.

Howard Hughes heard about the train and plane crashes on the local TV news. He summoned several of his associates, including his personal physician, and sent them to the hospital to consult with the doctors and administrators.

The photographer was Harry Watson, one of the Watson brothers who were legendary in news photography in southern California. Hughes didn't know that, nor did he care. All he knew was that a southern California photographer, maybe even the same one whom his bodyguards had ejected from the elevator a month or two earlier, was in critical condition, and Hughes marshaled all his resources to save his life. Perry Lieber, Hughes' faithful press liaison who spent the majority of his time keeping the boss' name out of the papers, never allowed a word to be breathed about what Hughes had done for Watson.

It was also Lieber who visited Watson's home and moved his wife and children to Las Vegas so they could be closer to Harry, who would remain in the hospital for almost a year. This was long before such things as group medical insurance and workman's compensation covered most of the expense of the treatment. No one ever knew how much it cost for Watson's time in the hospital and for his lengthy recuperation. But there were no bills to be paid by the family.

Harry Watson made several attempts to contact and thank Hughes, but was never able to do so.

At the end of his stay at the Flamingo, Hughes called Abe Schiller one morning, advised him that he was leaving the Flamingo that day, and asked that some special cartons and crates be sent to his wing for packing. At about noon on the same day, a caravan of moving vans pulled up in front of the Flamingo. Movers started carrying out all sorts of furniture, wardrobes, and unmarked crates and boxes. At the same time, Jimmy Vernon walked into Schiller's office, put a blank check on his desk, and asked him to write in the amount Hughes owed for the latest rent. Vernon also gave Schiller a list of furniture Hughes had decided he wanted to take along and told Schiller to add that to the hotel bill. After much scurrying and calculating, Schiller sought out Vernon, or anyone else in the Hughes entourage, to inform him of the total payment. But by then not a soul connected to Hughes could be found.

Among the items on the list of property taken by Hughes were 78 pink blankets. Schiller always wondered what use Hughes had for those blankets after he left the Flamingo.

Hughes didn't return to Las Vegas for nearly 15 years. And when he did, he bypassed the Flamingo in favor of the penthouse floor in a new tower of rooms at the Desert Inn. Hughes moved in and very little was heard from, or about, his party.

He continued to occupy the floor until Moe Dalitz, primary owner of the Desert Inn, needed the suites to accommodate high rollers over the upcoming Christmas and New Year's holidays, the biggest gambling period of the year. Hughes was paying top dollar for his digs, but it was still a gambling resort and Dalitz intended to take care of his best players.

Hughes sent word to Al Benedict, general manager of the Desert Inn, that he didn't want to move. Benedict consulted with Dalitz, who sent back a message advising Hughes that the only way he could stay in his quarters would be if he bought the whole property. Hughes responded with a purchase offer. Dalitz accepted. Hughes didn't have to move.

However, the state of Nevada was suddenly thrust into a state of turmoil. Gaming laws at the time limited licensing of casinos to individuals only. The state Gaming Control Board and the omnipotent Gaming Commission believed they were more effective at overseeing individuals than in chasing elusive public corporations if anything was amiss. This eliminated the possibility of organized crime figures setting up or buying into a corporation, then using it to run a casino.

So Howard Hughes could not buy the Desert Inn in the name of his Hughes Tool Company (later Summa Corporation). But he also wasn't about to file an application for a gaming license or submit to an extensive investigation by Nevada gaming regulators. He didn't want anyone snooping around in his business or personal affairs.

At the time, a variety of other pressure groups was lobbying to allow corporate licensing. Corporate America was chomping at the bit to get in on the growing action in Las Vegas. Our federal government was another entity in favor of changing the law: The feds were concerned with certain problems they could not totally eliminate because of the individual ownership laws. The feds were against licensing individuals only because, while they never wanted to admit it, the absence of corporate-style accounting and reporting allowed some of the criminal masterminds involved in hotel ownership to dance some fancy circles around the tax collectors.

The government agencies also believed that, by allowing publicly owned companies to be licensed as owners of casinos, the supposed "hoodlums" would be bought out by the faceless corporations, which enjoyed excellent public reputations.

On the other hand, many owners, bosses, workers, and observers within the gaming industry, including this writer, were against the idea of corporate ownership. We all shared the view of Chester Simms, as mentioned earlier, that gambling was far too personal a business to place it into the hands of accountants and computer geeks concerned primarily with reducing expenses and increasing profits.

But the evolution of the gambling industry could not be stopped. Reportedly, Governor Grant Sawyer, and his successor Paul Laxalt, were granted private audiences with Howard Hughes to discuss licensing. But sources close to Hughes maintain that those meetings never took place. Whether they did or didn't, both governors pressured the Nevada Legislature to enact new laws that would allow public corporations to own casinos.

In 1967, Hughes' Summa Corporation became the first to be granted such a license. Hughes was pleased. The corporations waiting in the wings were pleased. And the feds were particularly pleased. They'd been after Dalitz for nearly two decades, since his arrival in Nevada in 1950. And even though Dalitz's reputation in Las Vegas was that of a quiet friendly philanthropist who provided the majority of financial support for the Variety Club's School for Handicapped Children, the feds painted as nasty a portrait as possible of this alleged former boss of the deadly Purple Gang of Cleveland and Detroit. So of course, Moe was also pleased at the turn of events; by buying the Desert Inn,

Hughes had diverted the federal heat.

Once Hughes owned the DI, he had to manage it, so he hired former FBI agent and corporate security expert Robert Maheu to operate the property. While Maheu was busy trying to rectify the many procedural problems he found at the Desert Inn, Hughes was moving ahead and buying the Sands, the Frontier, the Silver Slipper, the Castaways, and the Landmark hotel-casinos in quick succession. He also tried to buy the Stardust, but federal anti-trust watchdogs from the Justice Department, worried that Hughes would end up with a monopoly in Las Vegas, prevented the sale from going through. Still, Hughes installed entirely new management teams in his six properties, and many of the new bosses had no casino management experience. For years it was chaos at the Summa Corporation casinos, and Hughes expected Maheu to oversee the staffs of the other joints in addition to handling his overwhelming duties at the Desert Inn.

Meanwhile, virtually every decision, expenditure, and tidbit of change had to be approved by Hughes, personally and directly. To make matters worse, Maheu had no access to Hughes, other than reaching him in his suite by phone or hand-written memo. And the ultra-private Hughes refused the majority of Maheu's calls. Maheu had to wait for Hughes to contact him in order to get a hearing on something that had to be done. Because Hughes was primarily a nocturnal creature, Maheu had to stay up all night, awaiting calls to discuss the need to repair the elevators at the Landmark or to redo a restaurant menu at the Frontier.

It was an impossible situation and the Hughes casinos hemorrhaged money for years. By the time he departed the Desert Inn in 1969, Hughes was in such poor physical condition that he couldn't have cared whether his businesses were turning a profit or not. He died a few years later. In time, the casinos were sold off by his estate. (Summa Corporation's last casino, Harold's Club in Reno, was sold to the Fitzgeralds group in 1988.)

No one at Summa would ever reveal just how many tens of millions of dollars the fabled Hughes fortune lost so Howard Hughes wouldn't have to move out of the Desert Inn.

Before He Was a Billionaire

In 1988 Summa sold the Desert Inn to another aviation pioneer and Las Vegas habitué who would also become a billionaire. To the uninitiated, he appeared to be just another well-mannered well-dressed young Flamingo crapshooter, whose handsome features, olive complexion, and streak of silver running through his jet-black hair made him look like a matinee idol.

But to those of us at the hotel, he was a truly nice guy whom we knew to be in the airplane business, salvaging old military planes to sell for parts, flying surplus bombers in the service of his fledgling air-freight operation, and building up a small fleet of DC-6Bs, one of the leading passenger planes of the era, for his non-scheduled charter flights.

His name was Kirk Kerkorian.

Kirk was a laid-back fellow who would hang around and shoot the breeze with dealers and pit bosses when he wasn't out on another trip to buy or sell or trade more planes. Being a Flamingo regular, Kerkorian drew the attention of Morris Lansburgh and his associates, who were starting to bring gamblers' junkets into Las Vegas from major cities around the country. Kerkorian cut a deal with

Lansburgh whereby his young Trans International Airlines would provide the flight service for the junkets.

At about the same time, the country was becoming embroiled in the Vietnam War. The military needed jet airliners to help transport troops and equipment to Southeast Asia. Kirk landed a major contract with the government, which he used as collateral to borrow $2 million for a down payment on a new Boeing 707 jetliner.

Suddenly Kerkorian didn't have time to hang around the crap tables socializing. His jet was continually commuting from the West Coast to Asia. His DC-6Bs were in the air most of the time, carrying load after load of Flamingo gamblers. His old bombers were delivering air freight around the world. Business was booming.

After a year or two, Morris Lansburgh called in Kerkorian and told him the Flamingo was happy with his service. However, the casino's customers no longer wanted to fly on the propeller-driven DC-6Bs. Instead, they wanted to travel on the new jets being introduced by all the major airlines.

Kerkorian needed the Flamingo account, but he couldn't come up with the $2 million down payment for another new jet. So he made Lansburgh an offer. If the Flamingo would invest the $2 million, Kirk would make the casino equal partners in his entire business. Though Lansburgh was ready to go for the deal, his associates in Miami gave it only the slightest consideration before instructing him to inform Kerkorian they didn't want to get into the airline business.

In a somewhat desperate move, Kerkorian traveled to his hometown of Fresno, California, where his family and most of his Armenian friends lived, hoping to raise some funds or at least get some advice. One of his Fresno pals, who worked for a brokerage firm, mentioned Kirk's dilemma to his company's development team and asked for suggestions. The answer came back: Take the airline public. Sell enough stock to raise the necessary capital to purchase the new jet and launch TIA as a full-blown charter airline.

Now all Kerkorian had to do was sell stock in his company; the price was $10 per share. He went to all his friends and relatives and implored them to buy in. Then it was back to Las Vegas, where he convinced a few hotel owners and executives to place orders for the stock. A newspaper columnist I know borrowed $10,000 on his home to buy a thousand shares. The swimming pool maintenance man at the Flamingo borrowed some money from a wealthy friend to get in on the offering.

The morning before the stock was to be issued, I was sitting in my office and overheard the conversation in which Kerkorian tried to convince Lansburgh to buy some shares. The Flamingo president hemmed and hawed and tried to explain that he never dabbled in new issues.

"You were the one most interested in spending the two million to buy half the airline and now you won't invest ten grand in it?" Kerkorian was dumbfounded. He finally shamed Lansburgh into picking up the phone and calling his broker to order a thousand shares. Immediately after Kerkorian left his office, however, Lansburgh was on the phone to Miami, laying off the stock on his partners.

Kirk's next move was to hire Bill Leonard, the sales director of Flying Tiger Airline, the leading charter carrier in the country. Then, he added Fred Benninger, the ultra hard-nosed businessman who called most of the shots at Flying Tiger. With Kerkorian in charge of the airplanes he knew so well and the two pros running the business, Trans International Airline became the new sweetheart of Wall Street's wisest investors. The TIA stock began flying higher and faster than the airplanes. Merger offers started streaming in.

Ultimately Kerkorian accepted an offer from United Artists, which bought up all the TIA stock at a price equal to $120 for each share that had been issued for $10. Kerkorian had become a very wealthy man. He still loved airplanes and air travel, so he and Benninger took the profits from TIA and bought Western Airlines, a major regional carrier ready to grow. But they didn't hold on to Western for very long. Again they accepted a spectacular merger offer and walked away with wheelbarrows full of greenbacks.

Meanwhile, back at the Flamingo, Morris Lansburgh and his partners were being hounded by the federal government on charges of skimming some $30 million off the top of Flamingo revenues, shorting Uncle Sam up to $10 million in taxes. The owners knew they had to sell and they were ready to part with the valuable hotel for a pittance.

Kerkorian, who by now was planning to build his own dream hotel called the International on land he owned next to the Las Vegas Convention Center, was interested in buying the Flamingo to use as a training location for his executive staff. He and Lansburgh hammered out a fantastic deal, where Kerkorian bought the entire property for about $15 million. The only condition was that the former owners would not open their books to the purchaser. But at such a bargain-basement price, Kerkorian didn't have to worry about records. The deal was done.

The International was built with money raised from a stock issued on the hotel itself. The property, the largest hotel in the world when it opened in 1969, was an immediate success. Kerkorian had attained the pinnacle of success in Las Vegas as the owner of two highly profitable major resorts.

Now it was time to find a new challenge. Metro

Goldwyn Mayer movie studios was on the sale block. Kirk thought the price was fair and MGM was suddenly his. But according to Dial Torgerson in his biography of Kerkorian, Kirk took his eye off the Las Vegas ball a little and found himself in some rare financial trouble.

Kerkorian had raised $30 million from a stock offering to build the International and fronted an additional $30 million out of his own pocket. He was planning to float another issue to recoup his own money, but he got into a jam with the feds over his refusal to show them the Flamingo's books (they were trying to pin something, anything, on Meyer Lansky). To retaliate, the SEC refused to let him float the second issue. Kerkorian, up to his neck in the MGM deal, got caught short on cash. He was forced to sell the Flamingo and the International to Hilton for what amounted to fifty cents on the dollar.

He also sold off the movie production and distribution units of MGM, but retained the MGM name and logo and trademarks, as well as the studio's old films. He put those assets to work when he built the MGM Grand Hotel, just down the Strip from the Flamingo. The MGM Grand was financed with yet another stock offering. Opened in 1973, it was the largest hotel in the world, several hundred rooms larger than his previous effort, which had been renamed the Hilton International.

The MGM Grand boasted attractions never before seen in Las Vegas. The stage spectacular, *Hello Hollywood*, produced by Donn Arden, was the most expensive extravaganza ever presented in a Las Vegas showroom; it featured a full-size jet airliner and a major flood on a gigantic stage that could do everything but walk and talk. The Grand introduced jai alai to Las Vegas and was the first local casino-hotel with a movie theater. Of course, it showed only MGM classics.

All in all, however, the MGM Grand was a fairly quiet resort. Neither Kerkorian nor Benninger was particularly publicity conscious, preferring to let their constantly improving earnings reports tell the story.

But then came the greatest disaster in Las Vegas history. In November 1980, a fire erupted in one of the MGM kitchens. Before it could be brought under control, flames and smoke had ingulfed the main building, killing 84 guests and employees and injuring 700 more.

Few observers believed Kerkorian and Benninger would rebuild the property, but they did. They built it exactly the same as the original structure and reopened to huge crowds. But those who knew the two men could see a change. They weren't as bright and eager with their new version of the MGM Grand. For years, the fire haunted the hotel, especially since new fire-safety standards enforced by the Clark County Fire Department had the MGM Grand name attached to them. So when Bally Manufacturing, at the time the world's largest manufacturer of slot machines, made a generous offer to buy the resort, Kerkorian and his stockholders collected their money. Kerkorian used some of the proceeds to become the largest stockholder in Chrysler Corporation, and that occupied his time for a while.

But he kept his eye on Las Vegas. A little more than 10 years later, he watched young Steve Wynn building his fancy Mirage Hotel and Casino, and Circus Circus putting up Excalibur which, with 4,000 rooms, would be the world's largest hotel.

Soon after the Mirage and Excalibur opened, Kirk Kerkorian announced his intention to build a new MGM Grand resort hotel at the intersection of the Las Vegas Strip and Tropicana Avenue, across the street from Excalibur. The MGM Grand would again be the largest resort in the world, with more than 5,000 rooms. And the new property would have a large amusement park, making it an option for the entire family.

Most people were shocked and amazed that Kerkorian, now well into his 70s and one of the richest individuals in the world, would undertake another huge challenge. While the experts were wondering why Kerkorian, who had certainly proved himself to the entire financial world, would take on such a massive new project, I wasn't at all surprised. Having known him for more than 30 years, I'd always found Kirk to be an even-tempered non-vindictive individual. However, I also thought that he still had to chafe over the way a very young Steve Wynn had made him look bad many years before.

In 1963, the vacant acreage on the northwest corner of the Strip and Flamingo Avenue, directly across from the Flamingo and the Dunes, became available for purchase. As previously mentioned, the Flamingo operators turned down the opportunity because of the dry wash that ran across the property.

While hanging around the Flamingo, Kerkorian heard the land was for sale. He wound up buying it for a very low price — because of the wash. When Nate Jacobson and Jay Sarno were getting ready to build Caesars Palace, they wanted the corner that Kirk owned. The location was ideal, and Kerkorian leased the land on which Caesars Palace would be built.

All went well until some time after Caesars Palace opened. Steve Wynn, the young owner of a liquor distributorship, called a press conference to unveil an artist's rendering of a small motel, slot machine arcade, and newsstand to be built on a tiny parcel of land directly alongside Caesars Palace.

The Caesars Palace developers went running to their landlord, Kirk Kerkorian, wanting to know why this piece of land wasn't included in what they were leasing. Kerkorian, like most everyone else in Las Vegas, had no idea where the parcel had come from. It turned out that the 40-foot-wide parcel was in the extreme northern corner of a piece of land the Dunes Hotel had given the state of Nevada to use for an off-ramp for the impending interstate highway. The parcel was in excess of what was needed for the ramp, so the Dunes sold the small plot to Howard Hughes' Summa Corporation.

It's been said that Jerry Zarowitz, one of the Caesars Palace owners at the time (and the man some have cited as one of Steve Wynn's mentors), learned about the property and suggested his young protege buy it. Wynn bought the parcel and immediately announced his project.

At the time, few believed Wynn ever intended to go ahead with the development. But the owners of Caesars Palace were in no position to risk having a grind joint attached like a tumor to their ultimate pleasure palace. They bought the land from Wynn for what was said to be a profit of at least a million dollars for the young entrepreneur, who used the money to begin buying up stock in the downtown Golden Nugget, the first building block in his casino empire.

But why would Zarowitz, an original owner of Caesars Palace, have informed Wynn of the availability of the small land parcel that could cause image problems for the big new hotel?

This was a tough time for Jerry Zarowitz. His qualifications as a casino operator were unchallenged, but Nevada authorities were questioning his association with some supposedly undesirable characters. Also, Zarowitz wasn't too pleased with some of the executives who had been brought in to run the property. Topping off his displeasure were the poor profits being turned in by the new casino, virtually from the day it opened. So in quick succession, Zarowitz was turned down for a gaming license, he immediately moved to Palm Springs to retire, and Steve Wynn wound up the owner of a little strip of coveted real estate.

As a result, Kerkorian was subjected to a lot of ridicule by the Caesars Palace operators, who reportedly used Kirk's error of omission to work out a lower purchase price when they eventually bought the Caesars Palace land from him. Ever since that time, some of us have believed that Kerkorian would one day repay Wynn. His announcement of the new MGM Grand took a lot of wind out of the sails of Treasure Island, the megaresort Wynn built next to the Mirage. And then Kerkorian hired Wynn's former general manager at the Golden Nugget, Bob Maxey, to be the president of the MGM Grand after Maxey and Wynn parted company.

Wynn, in turn, purchased the land where the Dunes Hotel and Country Club stood, beating out a bid for the property that had been made by Kirk Kerkorian. By the time he was through, Wynn owned almost all the land between Flamingo and Tropicana that butted up against Interstate 15. He also owned a large chunk of the ultra-valuable Strip frontage.

But then he ran into another roadblock with Kerkorian's name on it. Kirk bought a 20-acre parcel at the fourth corner of the Strip/Tropicana intersection, and immediately went into a joint venture with the Primm family to build another hotel-casino — New York-New York — on the property, making it forever unavailable to Wynn.

It's doubtful that the multibillionaire or the multimillionaire will ever publicly discuss their decades-long rivalry. But it's somewhat surprising that in the fairly tight gaming industry of southern Nevada, Kerkorian and Wynn don't seem to travel in the same circles.

Fathers and Sons

In Las Vegas' modern casino history, which dates back to 1931 when the state Legislature approved wide-open gambling, there have been some eminently successful family operations, with sons learning directly from their parents, then taking over the family empire. The best-known father-son tandems are Benny and Jack Binion, Sam and Bill Boyd, Jackie and Michael Gaughan, and the Frank Fertittas.

The Boyd family has been active in Nevada gambling for more than 40 years, ever since Sam, the family patriarch, decided to leave southern California, where his gambling activities were illegal, and join several of his friends in Las Vegas, where it wasn't. One of those friends was Milton Prell, owner of the Sahara, whom he joined on opening night. When Prell built the Mint Hotel in downtown Las Vegas, Boyd took over its operation.

Sam Boyd became an owner when he joined the group that built the Union Plaza in 1970. In 1979, Sam and his son Bill built the popular Sam's Town. Today the Boyd properties include the California, Main Street Station, and the Fremont in downtown Las Vegas, the Stardust on the Strip, the Eldorado and Joker's Wild in Henderson, and interests in Mississippi and Missouri.

The Boyd family boasts third-generation honors in Nevada gaming. Bill Boyd's son, William K., and his daughter, Marianne Boyd Johnson, both sit on the board of directors of the publicly traded corporation. As of this writing, Bill's son Sam is a casino shift manager at Sam's Town.

The Fertitta family has been involved in Nevada gambling for many years. Frank Fertitta, the father, was already well-established in the industry when Palace Station, then primarily a bingo hall, fell onto hard times because of problems involving some of its owners back in the days when the casino was called the Bingo Palace. Fertitta helped Palace Station get back on its feet, turning it into the protypical locals casino on Sahara Avenue just off the Strip. Any problems with the reputation of the property were wiped away by excellent service, low prices, and good food.

Frank Fertitta, the son, joined the firm, Station Casinos became a publicly traded corporation, and now Texas Station, Boulder Station, and Sunset Station dot the Las Vegas Valley. In addition, the corporation has spread across state lines and now operates in Missouri.

The Gaughan clan also boasts three generations in legal gambling, and four generations in the business. Preceding Jackie Gaughan, the current patriarch of the family's gaming operations in Nevada, was Jackie's father Michael, who was a partner with Ed Barrick and Sam Ziegman in a successful bookmaking operation in Omaha. When Barrick and Ziegman were invited to buy points in the proposed Flamingo Hotel in the mid-1940s, they offered a piece of the pie to Jackie's mother, who'd been recently widowed.

But Jackie learned the Nevada gambling business even before his mother bought into the Flamingo. During World War II, he was stationed in Tonopah, Nevada. On weekend passes, he'd join his buddies and take the 200-mile bus trip to Las Vegas, where he studied a form of gambling that he found much different from his father's illegal bookmaking.

At the end of the war, Jackie went to work as a dealer in the downtown casinos, furthering his education. When he returned home to Omaha, his mother suggested he go back to Las Vegas and work at the Flamingo to keep an eye on the family investment. Jackie and his wife Roberta moved their family to southern Nevada. He worked at the Flamingo, but his heart was downtown. No matter what his status, Jackie has always remained a down-home Cornhusker.

By the 1960s, the two-percent ownership held by the Gaughans was worth a lot of money. Son Michael was attending University of Southern California (USC) and Jackie insisted that he not fritter away his vacations, so Michael worked every summer at the Flamingo while in college. He was accorded no special treatment.

Jackie and his old friend, Mel Exber, joined forces and in 1961 took over the Las Vegas Club, a casino created more for the sportsman than for the usual gambler. Both men have always been great sports fans and it was Exber who was the driving power in the lengthy, but successful, effort to bring Class AAA baseball to town in the form of the Las Vegas Stars.

In 1964, Jackie got his ducks in a row, sold off the family's interest in the Flamingo, and began negotiating the purchase of the venerable El Cortez Hotel and Casino, one of the oldest gaming properties in Las Vegas. Located three blocks from the concentration of casinos that make up Glitter Gulch, the El Cortez had one old depressing building with a small casino and a few dozen hotel rooms. But Jackie had enough money to buy the place and spruce it up. He expanded the casino and added a new tower. Today, the old wing, which was built in 1941, is the oldest original casino building in the country.

When federal authorities learned that Jackie Gaughan had applied for a gaming license for the El Cortez, they went running to Carson City and pleaded with state gaming regulators to attach a proviso to the license: that Jackie Gaughan open separate bank accounts for the business and for himself. The condition was attached and, for the first time in his life, Jackie Gaughan had a bank account. Prior to that time, he paid for everything with cash and didn't keep books.

Rumor has it that there was a giant celebration in Washington the night it was announced that various federal agencies could now keep tabs on the elusive businessman. It should also be noted that in the more than 30 years since Gaughan was forced to set up those accounts, there has never been a hint of impropriety in his dealings.

Jackie was always his own best public-relations man. He would leave his cubbyhole office at the El Cortez each morning with his pockets stuffed full of coupons for free meals, free drinks, free nickels, and anything else he could think of to give away. Soon every motel owner and employee got to know Jackie Gaughan as he visited the scores of motels around Las Vegas on a daily basis and dropped off stacks of tickets for the operators to give to their guests. The guests would turn them in for all sorts of goodies at the El Cortez, where they would feel welcome and do a bit of gambling.

Michael watched his father — and others — very closely. During his years working at the Flamingo, Michael accepted any and all work, even menial positions, and never openly complained. There was no doubt in the minds of anyone who knew him what the future held for Michael Gaughan.

Not long after his graduation from USC with a degree in business administration, Michael felt prepared to enter the gaming business on his own. He partnered up with a group of young men who'd all been good friends since childhood. With Michael in the lead, they bought the small Royal Hotel and Casino off the Strip near the Convention Center. They invested their savings, worked hard, and became successful casino operators.

When Michael first came up with the idea to build the Barbary Coast, he wanted to place it at the corner of Flamingo Road and the Strip. The Flamingo was about 60 feet from the corner, with the Desert Villa Motel firmly planted right at the intersection. Much as they tried, Michael and his real estate agents couldn't get the owner of the motel to even consider a sale. Out of frustration, Michael mentioned it to his father. In less than a week, Jackie called his son and asked if he would like to talk about leasing the property; Jackie had purchased the parcel from the owner, who was an old friend. To this day, Michael pays his father rent for the land that some hotel owners now consider the most valuable tract on the Strip.

The relatively small Barbary Coast squats between the giant Flamingo and the giant Bally's, sharing the corner of Flamingo Road and the Strip with Caesars Palace and the new Bellagio. It's a miniature casino compared to the behemoths surrounding it, but Michael Gaughan's small joint gets a crack at players occupying nearly 20,000 rooms within a hundred yards of the place.

Once the Barbary Coast was launched and sailing briskly, Michael and his partners poured their profits into building the Gold Coast Hotel and Casino, located on Flamingo Road about a mile west of the Barbary Coast. To attract the local trade, they added such amenities as a movie theater, bowling lanes, a big buffet, and plenty of free parking. The bingo parlor is so large that it had to be built on a mezzanine level.

Most of Michael's partners from the Barbary Coast joined him at the Gold Coast, then joined him again at the the Orleans. The latter is another favorite of the locals: it offers a bowling alley, big movie theater, great buffet, showroom, poker room, lots of positive-return video poker, and a huge parking lot.

Jackie also caters to the local trade and does a fabulous amount of business every year. Both Gaughans believe in continuous promotion and both know how to strike the right nerve to draw more and more customers into their casinos:

Each offers several near-giveaway food specials in their restaurants; each keeps cocktail prices very low; each provides guest rooms in their hotels at bargain prices; and each offers slot machines with about the lowest house percentage in Las Vegas. But when they get together, they disagree on virtually everything that has to do with operating successfully in the gaming industry.

It has been speculated that father and son are so much alike that it's difficult for them to get along. While there is great love and respect between the two men, any attempt to discuss business situations deteriorates into a shouting match, with each trying to convince the other that he's wrong.

The rivalry between father and son has been healthy, as far as business in concerned, for them as well as for the entire gaming industry. Master promoters both, they come up with new crowd-attracting features on a nearly daily basis. Other casino owners watch the moves made by the Gaughans, allowing father and son to work out the bugs before implementing the perfected promotion. But as soon as the competition picks up on one Gaughan deal, Jackie or Michael comes up with something new.

And now, Michael's three sons—John, Michael, and Brendan—are grown and working in their father's casinos.

11

The Stardust

When I first started working at the Flamingo in 1960, I was 27 years old, the youngest PR man in Las Vegas at the time. I worked there until 1967, when Las Vegas' world began turning upside down.

With the Nevada laws altered to allow public corporations to hold gaming licenses, and emboldened by the Moe Dalitz-Howard Hughes deal for the Desert Inn, the federal authorities believed they could start making decisive moves in Las Vegas. After all, the corporations were ready and able to buy out the old owners with their questionable associations. One of the first investigations launched by the feds was into the skimming of gambling revenues at the Flamingo. It was a slam dunk: They had enough information on so many owners and executives that they were able to offer to trade immunity for testimony.

Once the Flamingo principals started feeling some pressure, they began looking for their own buyer. In 1966, the Flamingo started negotiations with Sheraton Corporation, which had lined up a Japanese billionaire who wanted to buy the resort and have Sheraton operate it for him. Everything went well until state authorities explained that the Japanese investor would have to be licensed as the owner, while Sheraton would be issued the permit as the operator. With all the heat around the Flamingo, the investor decided to get out of the kitchen — and the country. That's when the feds and their strike force started playing hardball with the Flamingo owners, which resulted in the quick sale to Kirk Kerkorian. Kerkorian, of course, was clean, and had no trouble getting licensed again.

While Lansburgh was negotating with Sheraton, I decided it would be an excellent time to leave town. I was tired of watching federal agents sweeping through the hotel. I was also tired of dealing with some of the spoiled entertainers who appeared in our showroom. For some reason, the so-called stars who caused the most problems for the resort staff were always the ones whose acts bombed. In short, I was tired of the whole scene.

I went to Lansburgh and told him I'd be leaving on the date that Sheraton intended to take over the Flamingo: April 1, 1967. April Fool's Day.

In early March, Lansburgh stopped by my office and informed me that the deal with Sheraton had fallen through. I left town anyway, moving my family back to southern California, where I opened my own public-relations business.

Meanwhile, a stack of documents was filed in federal court charging Lansburgh, partner Sam Cohen, and some of the other point holders and executives of participating in skimming activities that allegedly totaled more than $25 million during the period they operated the Flamingo. Some of the bosses served six months to a year in federal custody; most of them were incarcerated at what was known as the "federal country club" at Egland Air Force Base in Florida.

Lansburgh, however, was totally shocked when his

number was finally called. He thought the early convictions would be the only ones, but the feds saved Lansburgh and Cohen for last. Since Lansburgh always attempted to divorce himself from casino activities, he couldn't understand why he was being charged with participating in the skim. However, the prosecution maintained that in the seven years Lansburgh had been the actual operator of the resort, he had to have known large portions of the profits were sent to Meyer Lansky and his people in Florida on a regular basis. The feds hoped that either Lansburgh or Cohen would incriminate Lansky, the ultimate target of the federal task force. But both men kept quiet and served their six months.

Lansburgh was released from prison a broken man. He returned to his Miami Beach resort properties and literally worked himself to death, because of the shame he felt over his conviction. He ran back and forth among his eight hotels on a daily basis and usually didn't get home until the wee hours. He kept up the torrid pace for less than a year, and then he was found slumped over the steering wheel of a recently acquired Rolls-Royce, dead of a heart attack.

Tony Cornero

Things went along nicely for me and my PR firm for nearly four years, until I got a phone call from Norris Goldman, the new president of Recrion Corporation in Las Vegas, the company that owned the Stardust, Fremont, and Aladdin. I knew Nor from my Flamingo days; his father Harry Goldman had been partners with Al Parvin, who bought the Flamingo after Greenbaum's group left, and owned Parvin-Dohrmann hotel suppliers and builders. Nor made me an offer I couldn't refuse to be marketing director of Recrion Corporation, so I closed my office and dragged the family back to Vegas. This was in 1971. My office was at the Stardust.

The Stardust's story is long and sordid. It began in the early 1950s, when an Italian dreamer named Tony Cornero was busy finalizing plans for his own hotel and casino. It would be like nothing Las Vegas had ever seen.

Cornero was well-known in southern California as the owner and operator of the *Lux*, a luxurious gambling ship anchored off the coast of Los Angeles, just beyond the three-mile line that was said to be the beginning of international waters. The *Lux* could be seen from Santa Monica Beach and thousands of Los Angeles-area residents crowded the water taxis to get to the ship each day. Cornero's *Lux* and a few other gambling ships and barges flourished until the state of California got the federal government to agree that the three-mile limit off the Pacific coast did not demarcate international waters. The winning argument was based on the fact that Catalina Island, 26 miles across the San Pedro Channel, was a part of Los Angeles County. Therefore, the waters off the Los Angeles County coast could not be considered international.

Cornero made a feeble attempt to haul the *Lux* up the coast, beyond Los Angeles County. However, Ventura and Santa Barbara counties claimed the Anacapa Islands, which were far enough away to put the *Lux* out of business.

But Cornero wasn't slowed by any of this. He had a dream: to build the largest resort hotel in Las Vegas. His place would sport 1,500 rooms, while the largest property at the time had a mere 200. Furthermore, while the average room rate in Las Vegas in the mid-1950s was about $12 per night, Cornero was going to offer rooms for $5.

Tony the Dreamer had only one problem: financing. He'd always operated as a loner. His legal battles to keep his gambling ship afloat had tapped him out. He had to raise a stake.

A native of Italy, Cornero was still fluent in the mother language and had come to know many first-generation Americans. He also knew their parents and could converse with them about the old country over traditional Italian dinners. As Cornero enjoyed the hospitality of the Los Angeles Italian community, he regaled his friends with the story of his planned Las Vegas resort. He showed them artists' renderings and plans and built up a storm of excitement among his countrymen.

Cornero started selling stock at $5 a share. The response was enthusiastic. Cash in hand, he returned to Las Vegas and hired the contractors. Ground was broken with great fanfare and construction began. The contractors on the Stardust project insisted on cash in advance before putting their men out on the job. They knew that once the building crews got to work, Cornero would take the opportunity to relax a bit. That meant walking across the Strip from his construction site and into the posh Desert Inn, where he'd stop at his favorite dice table, pull a wad of hundreds from his pocket, and fire it up.

Throughout his gambling career, Cornero made money at the crap table only from the custodial side. He rarely walked away from a dice-shooting session with any cash.

The Stardust rose from the desert for about two weeks on Cornero's initial bankroll. But the rest of his capital disappeared into the Desert Inn's cage. Try as he might to convince the builders to carry him, they wouldn't budge. He offered them thousands of shares of stock in the hotel, but they had to have cash to meet their payrolls and purchase their supplies.

So Cornero caught the first plane to Los Angeles. Now he had all sorts of pictures to show his stockholders — and prospective stockholders. They saw photos of Cornero shaking hands with the governor, both U.S. senators from Nevada, the state's only congressman, and numerous local dignitaries who'd turned out for the groundbreaking. Another stack of photos showed workers digging ditches and pouring concrete. On the strength of this photographic evidence, Cornero collected cash and issued receipts to new investors to whom he would send his attractive stock certificates. Most of his investors were men and women who owned their own small businesses, mainly in the downtown area and in the eastern end of Los Angeles. Cornero's pictures and his glib tongue convinced these simple folk that their investments of a few hundred or a few thousand dollars in a Las Vegas resort-casino would provide their families with the luxuries they would never be able to afford in any other way.

Cornero assured them that virtually every resort and casino in Las Vegas had more than paid for itself within two years of opening. The dividends flowed freely to the pointholders. He'd read an article about General Motors' stock and used it to illustrate how a hundred dollars invested in his company at the outset could be worth tens of thousands of dollars. That got their attention. Then he moved in for the kill, explaining that anyone who'd bought and held a thousand dollars worth of GM stock was now a millionaire. Once the fantasy took hold, the money was quick in coming.

His pockets filled again, Cornero returned to Las Vegas, gave the contractors some more cash, and went back to relaxing at the Desert Inn crap tables.

He repeated this routine at least a half-dozen times. Still, the hotel was less than half completed. After coming back from one of his selling sojourns, Cornero didn't appear to be himself. He was still dapper, but his gait was a bit slower and he didn't have the usual spring in his step. He was quiet and subdued. Some speculated that Cornero was finally feeling the ill effects of taking millions of dollars from his trusting countrymen without much hope of ever being able to repay them.

Fact was, Tony the Dreamer had more serious problems: He was breaking federal and state laws all over the place. He hadn't gone to the trouble of registering his stock offerings with the Securities and Exchange Commission. Nor had he taken into account the fact that, according to state law, every one of his thousands of investors had to be licensed as an owner of a gambling establishment. He hadn't kept very good track of whom he'd sold the stock to or for how much. And, of course, the contractors were demanding more cash up front before they'd go back to work.

Cornero crossed the street to the Desert Inn for another dice session. His wallet was thinner than usual, but he was again confident he could beat the dice. He was actually a few thousand ahead when he quietly started sliding toward the floor. No one noticed anything different—until one of the dealers peered over the table and said, "Hey, Mr. C is down. Maybe there's something wrong."

Someone called for an ambulance. A worker in the casino cage produced a blanket, which was placed over him. Then, as usual, the game went on. Players stepped over his prone body to pass by. By the time the ambulance arrived, Tony Cornero was dead from a heart attack.

A huge legal battle ensued over his estate and the still-uncompleted Stardust Hotel. All of the stockholders wanted to ensure their positions. There were no creditors, since whatever work was done had been pre-paid in cash. When the dust settled and the attorneys had collected their fees, the shareholders learned their stock was completely worthless.

The hotel property was turned over to the Desert Inn

owners, who paid off Cornero's personal debts in return for clear title to the property. The DI ownership then went to work completing the Stardust just as Cornero had planned.

When the hotel opened in 1958, most local casino properties were catering to big players. But the Stardust managers made it known that they were aiming for the blue-collar crowd. One of the first things they did was install signs and bright lights throughout the huge casino. Previously, lighted signs weren't seen inside any Nevada casino. Then the managers opened a low-priced buffet, serving breakfast, lunch, and dinner; the evening meal was the most expensive at about a buck and a half. Keno, a popular game in downtown casinos, hadn't been seen on the Strip until the Stardust included it in the roster of games. The biggest difference, though, was in the number of slot machines. While all other Strip casinos had a dozen or fewer one-armed bandits, the Stardust opened with nearly a hundred.

It worked. In its first year of operation, the Stardust was the top moneymaking hotel-casino in all of Nevada, and it held that position for many years. Still, the original stockholders never saw a single cent of those profits, which dwarfed even Cornero's predictions. Most of the money went to the Chicago mob.

The Stardust was still filling coffers in Chicago when I went to work there for Norris Goldman.

Goldman and Sachs

A couple of months after I arrived, Nor Goldman put a gun to his head and committed suicide in the bedroom of his Beverly Hills home. Almost from the day he assumed the presidency of Recrion Corporation and took the reins as CEO of the Stardust Hotel, his personality changed.

He was getting telephone calls several times a day from Del Coleman, a major stockholder in Recrion and a liaison for the true owners of the corporation in Chicago. Coleman was second-guessing Goldman on virtually every move he made at the Stardust, Fremont, and Aladdin. Goldman was a serious businessman who was working hard to prove to his father, another large shareholder, that he could operate a major casino. But the Coleman phone calls wouldn't let up. Goldman resorted to visiting a psychiatrist. The doctor told him he had to relax a little and not let the telephone calls bother him.

Goldman finally called me and another corporate executive, who was also a good friend, into his office. He explained what had been happening and told us he would take the advice of his psychiatrist and spend less time at the hotels. He asked each of us to keep him informed of any situations we thought he should know about. But a couple of week later, he succumbed to the pressure and blew his brains out.

One day after the funeral, the Recrion board of directors named Allen D. Sachs the new president of Recrion and chief executive of the Stardust. Sachs had been the casino manager at the Stardust for a couple of years. But he'd been a part of Moe Dalitz's organization for a lot longer, having begun his casino career as a dealer at the Desert Inn. Over the years, he proved to be a most capable and loyal employee and worked his way up through the casino ranks. Dalitz kept his eye on Sachs, whom he finally appointed manager of the huge casino at the Stardust.

Once Sachs was in place in the executive office, I went to him and offered to leave my position at his will. He and

I didn't really know each other; I'd been brought in by Nor Goldman, a different type of businessman than Sachs. So I felt it proper to offer to step out of the way, allowing Sachs to make his own appointment to the top marketing position. He thanked me for the offer and said he would consider it.

Sachs never did ask me to leave. In fact, we worked well together for four years. We designed promotional and advertising campaigns and established Stardust Camperland, the first recreational-vehicle park connected with a major resort-casino.

Though Recrion and some of its early owners were in the midst of problems with the federal government over allegations of irregularities in their business practices, the corporation was successful and making a lot of money.

In fact, this was becoming a problem: Recrion was making too much money. To disburse some cash from the corporation, the executive officers and major shareholders tampered with the stock. A solid $20-a-share stock would suddenly spike up to $150 a share. This was repeated two or three times before the Securities and Exchange Commission caught on. Probably as much to cover up its own sloppy handling of the situation as to penalize the wrongdoing, instead of bringing the Recrion principals to trial, the SEC issued a consent decree, preventing certain shareholders from selling their Recrion stock publicly or privately. The only way the principals could ever get any money out of their shares was to liquidate the company.

Thus, Recrion was put up for sale.

A couple of months after I was informed that the corporation would be sold to bail out the largest stockholders, I was called into Al Sachs' office and given information to be released on the sale of Recrion to Argent Corporation. I dutifully produced the news release and distributed it throughout the country. The head of Argent was Allen Glick, and the fireworks were about to begin.

Argent Arrives on the Scene

It all started with Allen Glick. Glick was a young go-getter who did a tour of duty in Vietnam, held a license to practice law in Pennsylvania, and had a great appetite for success. He later joined a real-estate firm in San Diego and became a business superstar in a relatively short time. Glick, who had no "connections," began hanging around La Costa Country Club, just north of San Diego. At the time, big-money men, a lot of them sporting names that ended in vowels, regularly spent time at the posh club, which had been built with money from the Teamsters Union at the same time that the union's pension fund was financing new casinos in Las Vegas.

Hanging around La Costa, Glick got to know many of the members. One of his new friends was Eugene Fresch, who'd made his money manufacturing armaments. Soon, word got to Glick that the Hacienda Hotel in Las Vegas was for sale by the estate of the late Judy Bayley. The numbers looked good to the real-estate man, so he and Fresch visited Las Vegas and began working on a deal. The sale was finalized in 1971. Glick and Fresch had no difficulty in obtaining their Nevada gaming licenses. Both men were squeaky clean.

Glick's arrival on the Las Vegas scene was a non-event. The Hacienda stood all alone at the far south end of the Strip and wasn't a particularly bright star in the Las Vegas firmament. However, Glick, Fresch, and their investors seemed content. And why wouldn't they be? The percentage of return on a casino operation was far better than that of stocks, bonds, or real estate. Glick's own star was rising at La Costa, where he rubbed elbows with other Las Vegas casino owners who visited the resort on a regular basis.

Meeting Glick for the first time was also a non-event. He was a bald, owlish, little man who didn't strike me as a potential heavyweight in the rough-and-tumble gambling business. I saw a pleasant-enough 32-year-old fellow who would do as he was told by the Chicago underworld. The bosses got their money out of the stock from the sale of Recrion to Argent, but they still retained hidden ownership and control of the Stardust and Fremont — and now the Hacienda.

I interviewed Glick in preparation for writing a bio to put out to the news media introducing them to the Stardust's new owner. His answers to my questions were almost laughable. Glick told me a fairy tale about his takeover of Recrion Corporation. That story is related for the first time here, since I refused ever to write a news release based on such dubious facts.

Glick told me that when he heard Recrion was up for sale, he went directly to Recrion's majority stockholder, Del Coleman, in Chicago, and proposed a purchase. Coleman was a suave capable individual who was also tough enough to represent the Teamsters Union and the Chicago mob in their Las Vegas business affairs.

Glick had never met Coleman, but according to Glick's tale, the tough Chicago businessman took an immediate liking to him and offered to sell him Recrion. The assets of the corporation were close to $200 million, which would be the sale price. Coleman told Glick he'd accept a $2 million down payment to close the deal.

"Two million dollars for a two-hundred-million-dollar corporation?" I asked, eyebrows raised.

"That's right," Glick answered. "One percent down."

Then, according to Glick, he left Coleman's Chicago office, went to the airport, and caught a plane to Tennessee. There, young Allen went to a bank and met a banker, also for the first time. This banker admired Glick's spunk, so he loaned him the two million on the spot.

How did Glick happen to pick this particular bank in Tennessee and then happen to reach the one man who could immediately approve a loan of $2 million? I was never told. But Glick reported that he returned to Chicago, went to Coleman's office, and delivered the $2 million. He became the new owner of a $200 million corporation without putting up one cent of his own money. The deal was made and everyone lived happily ever after. At least that was the end of the story Glick would have had me believe.

Of course, some fairy tales don't always turn out that way. Too often a tall menacing villain with thin lips and hooded eyes, and dressed all in black, enters the picture. The villain proceeds to wreak havoc with the wonderful little people who are trying to play their wonderful little parts in the wonderful little story. When Glick walked into the Stardust, he announced his first executive appointment: Frank "Lefty" Rosenthal would be his chief aide.

Rosenthal was to work in the poker room as a "coordinator." What that title was supposed to mean, no one could ever figure out. It seemed that Rosenthal was spending a lot more time in the executive offices than in the poker room. It didn't take long for me to come to the conclusion that he was actually in the Stardust to keep an eye on it for the Chicago bosses.

However, because of Rosenthal's unsavory reputation, not to mention a criminal conviction for fixing college basketball games (conveniently expunged from the records before his arrival in Las Vegas), Nevada gaming authorities immediately declared that he could not hold an administrative position or make any administrative decisions until he was approved for a gaming license as a key employee.

Lefty was above all that. He began calling the shots at both the Stardust and the Fremont. He convened major staff meetings, during which Allen Glick and the other executives of the hotels sat at a long head table while Rosenthal dictated policy.

When Rosenthal took charge, I got ready to bail out. I came to know him, somewhat, as he roamed through the casino or held court at a vacant table in the poker room. I found him to be a cold man who seemed to have an awful lot on his mind. I didn't care for him and wanted nothing to do with him. I think it's safe to say the feeling was mutual.

Employees throughout the Stardust came to fear the sight of the tall man with the Louis Roth suits and rapidly thinning straw-colored hair. They never knew when he might call their number and put them out of work.

I didn't harbor such fears. I knew I couldn't stay at the Stardust much longer. I foresaw Rosenthal bringing great embarrassment to the legalized gaming industry of Nevada, so to gather evidence, I began collecting data on his activities, which included tape recordings of some of those staff meetings.

During the seven years I'd been employed at the Flamingo, I realized that there was underworld ownership and control, but I was never asked (or told) to work directly with the mob's lieutenants. I was allowed to do my job without interference or intimidation. But within minutes of the Argent takeover of Recrion, I knew there was no way I'd be able to work with these people. I seriously considered handing in my resignation, but then decided I would remain until they fired me.

Why? For one thing, I knew the longer I stayed, the more I'd learn, which would probably come in handy later on. Also, I wanted to hold on—just for spite.

During my years with Recrion, I'd established the first in-house advertising agency in a Las Vegas resort. Through our Lodestar Advertising, we were able to place all advertising for our properties and keep the sizable commissions paid to the agencies. Lodestar maintained a large bank balance of commission money, which was periodically transferred to the parent corporation. Rosenthal learned of this pot of gold and wanted it. However, the money could not be released to anyone but the parent corporation without approval from our comptroller and me. When Glick arrived, there was more than a million dollars in the account, and I waited for the powers that be to either ask me to sign for the transfer of the money or boot me out. They chose the latter.

When the day finally arrived for them to get rid of me, they passed the responsibility to Herb Tobman, the Stardust's vice president. They were keeping Tobman around until they learned the inner workings of the property (then they dumped him, too). Their timing was well-planned. Al Sachs, still president of the Stardust, was in France working to renew the contract for *Lido de Paris*, the resort's spectacular nightclub revue. (Once Sachs returned from Europe, he too was sent packing.)

When Tobman informed me that the new brass wanted me to resign, I told him I would leave, but I wouldn't quit; my resignation could be tendered only if I thought I couldn't do my work. Because I could still do the job I'd been doing with some success for the past four years, I insisted on being terminated.

"You go back to Lefty," I patiently explained, "and tell him I won't quit. I want to be fired."

Tobman nodded his head and left. A few minutes later he returned and tried to explain that Rosenthal would rather I resign than make me carry the stigma of having been fired. Since I didn't think it was a stigma to let it be known I was in no way connected with this organization, I again asked him to fire me.

Rosenthal, through Tobman, finally did. I removed all my company credit cards and handed them to the vice president, along with the keys to the company car and my office. I then produced a list I had prepared for this moment and had him sign a receipt for everything I'd handed him.

I asked for fifteen minutes to clear out my own things, which he granted. I slid behind my typewriter, wrote a news release on my firing, and made arrangements to have it distributed.

Walking away from the Stardust was a relief. I sensed that something very bad would happen before too long. I drove home and picked up my wife Joyce and a suitcase. Once we were back in the car, I asked where she wanted to go. I really didn't care; all I wanted was a few days to lie back and breathe. A trip to San Diego did the job. We returned and started taking stock of our situation. I'd been in the gaming industry for almost 15 years, working six or seven days and almost as many nights each week. Vacations had been few and far between. Maybe it was time to relax for a while.

But that wasn't to be. Almost immediately after returning home from San Diego, I learned that some false stories about me were being circulated around Las Vegas. I wanted to respond, but felt thwarted because I had no forum in which to do so. That's when serendipity took over once again.

I received a lunch invitation from my old friend Bob Brown, a veteran newspaper reporter and publisher. Bob had just purchased the sleepy little *North Las Vegas Valley Times* newspaper, had converted it from a weekly to a daily, and was ready to take on the competition of the established *Review-Journal* and the *Sun*. Bob had read the press release about my leaving Argent Corporation and wanted me to do some writing for his paper. For me, the real fun was about to begin.

12

The Newspapermen

It had to be one of the biggest and best days in the lives of Hank and Barbara Greenspun, owners and publishers of the *Las Vegas Sun*. It was early 1953 and they had just returned from federal court, where they'd won a lawsuit they'd filed against Nevada's senior U.S. senator, Pat McCarran, and a long list of resort hotels, charging them all with an illegal boycott. It was alleged that McCarran had induced the hotel owners to pull all their advertising from Greenspun's struggling young newspaper because of some nasty editorial comments Greenspun had hurled at the senator. And now the publisher and his wife had emerged victorious against one of the most powerful men not only in the state, but also in the entire country.

Greenspun had arrived in Las Vegas to run a daily newspaper under the auspices of the International Typographical Union. The union was intent on trying to break the established *Review-Journal*, whose publisher, Don Reynolds, refused to recognize the union when it tried to organize the printers. The union was publishing a daily called the *Las Vegas Free Press*; Greenspun changed the name to the *Las*

Vegas Sun.

So there was Greenspun with a new daily newspaper, trying to compete with a long-established paper in a town with a total population of about 30,000. He was determined to establish the *Sun* as a champion of the people, fighting against the establishment. He tilted at windmills in every edition.

Greenspun's win over the McCarran forces put the *Sun* on the map in Nevada. But it was his almost single-handed fight against Senator Joseph McCarthy and his "Red Scare" that deposed the controversial politician from Wisconsin. Greenspun dug up facts that would have made today's scandal magazines blush and used them in his columns, which circulated all over the nation's capital. Suddenly Hank Greenspun was recognized as a newspaper publisher who was not to be trifled with. In the more than 30 years that he led his paper, no one could ever accuse him of being a "good old boy." Greenspun was born to battle the good old boys.

Winning his lawsuit against McCarran and the hotels was a huge victory. It provided the Greenspuns with badly needed capital to keep their newspaper printing on a daily basis; equally important, it gave Hank a much loftier status in this town, where rank counts for everything.

Greenspun always championed the underdog. He was an attorney in New York City prior to arriving in Las Vegas. During that time, Israel was granted its independence and various Arab nations were poised to go to war against the new country. Greenspun, along with many other young Jewish men, was accused of smuggling munitions to Israel, a "crime" for which he was later thanked by the Jewish state and pardoned by President John Kennedy. But he lost his right to practice law in New York. So he turned to the newspaper business.

In the early days, it was essentially Greenspun's upstart

Sun versus the *Review-Journal* and its peppery owner, Don Reynolds. Reynolds figured that Clark County couldn't support two dailies, especially since that new invention called television was already beginning to seduce readers away from newspapers all over the country. A product of the "old school" in Nevada, Reynolds battled Greenspun tooth and nail. The competition actually strengthened both newspapers, and ultimately Reynolds branched out. Today, Donrey Enterprises encompasses newspapers, and radio and TV stations throughout the country, along with outdoor advertising companies and a variety of other communication-oriented businesses.

During his meteoric ascent, Don Reynolds never changed. He was a humble man, proud of his background and his roots. Throughout his lifetime, his newspapers practiced what the boss preached. You would have been hardpressed to find a Donrey newspaper ever printing scandalous news. Reynolds, a caring man, would not stoop to the base desires of some readers to increase his newspaper sales.

My favorite story about Don Reynolds occurred shortly after I had joined the staff at the Flamingo. One afternoon as I sat in my office, Reynolds paid me a surprise visit. I was used to being called on by Fred Smith, an advertising sales representative from the *R-J*, or members of the editorial department. But a visit by Reynolds himself was a big deal. I immediately went out to see him.

After the greetings, Reynolds invited me to have a drink with him to celebrate "the most important day" of his life. Who was I to refuse? We went into the Driftwood Lounge and ordered cocktails. I was burning to know what he was celebrating, and he told me.

Reynolds had just come from the mortgage company where he'd made the final payment on the GI home he'd bought just after he was mustered out of the service at the end of World War II. The home, in the Twin Lakes area of Las Vegas, had cost him $8,000. He was near tears as he set down his glass, reached into his pocket, and pulled out the deed to the house.

"It's all paid for, Dick," he uttered with pride. "In all these years I've never missed a single payment." The fact that Reynolds had not lived in the tract house for many years, having long since moved to a huge mansion in the hills overlooking Las Vegas, didn't mean a thing. His original homestead was now all his, and he retained ownership of it until his death.

To his dying day, Don Reynolds continued to insist that Las Vegas had room for only one daily newspaper. Hank Greenspun demonstrated successfully that there was room for two. And then along came Bob Brown, proclaiming that he would start up a third daily paper in town. No one ever doubted Bob, who was known and respected throughout the state. One of the most honest and devoted men I've ever known, Bob was a newspaperman by trade. But more important, he was a source of solid counsel to those who wanted to serve their communities.

Brown had originally come to Las Vegas in the 1940s, when he wrote for, and later edited, the *Review-Journal*. He also got involved in Nevada politics and served terms on the State Tax Commission, the predecessor to the Gaming Commission and Gaming Control Board. In addition, he helped establish a few advertising agencies in town. But Bob had a wanderlust that seems to be part of the personality of many newsmen.

He left Las Vegas and published newspapers all the way from northern New England to Washington state. In each case, he would eventually sell out and return to Las Vegas. While Bob was a premier newsman, he was a rotten businessman and always wound up making little or no money on his ventures. His final attempt at publishing turned out to be the *North Las Vegas Valley Times,* a weekly paper that Bob converted to six days a week. In the relatively short life span of the *Valley Times,* the paper served the people of Nevada very well, primarily because of Bob Brown's straightforward approach to the news.

Bob was getting his paper off the ground at the same time the bosses of Argent decided they didn't want me aboard any longer. Newly unemployed, I accepted an invitation to meet with my old friend. Bob and I had lunch at the Las Vegas Country Club and talked for hours; we didn't leave our table until the dinner crowd began arriving. Bob's major problem was establishing a defined niche in the market for his *Valley Times.* He had to show that his paper was completely different from the *Review-Journal* and the *Sun.*

One thing he did was cover the gambling industry in more detail than either of the other papers had ever done. He sent members of his limited staff to cover meetings of the State Gaming Control Board and Gaming Commission. At that time, industry news was generally ignored by the other papers, which were content to rake in huge profits from the casinos each month and wanted no part in possibly rocking their own boat.

Bob wanted me to help him cover the casinos.

My objection that I'd been away from the newspaper business for too long just didn't cut it with Bob. He'd thought it all out before he invited me to lunch. He wanted to be the only newspaper in the state that did a thorough and honest job of reporting on the gaming industry.

"Every paper in Nevada prints puff pieces for the casinos," Bob began, telling me what I already knew. "They pretty well have an unwritten agreement in which the papers promise to write only what the hotels and casinos want them to. In return, they receive their big advertising schedules and all those dollars."

Then he shuddered slightly. "I don't want to sell out and be just another whore newspaper. I want to give my readers whatever the news really is, no matter what the advertising situation might be." He slapped the table in what amounted to the greatest display of anger or emotion I'd ever seen from this mild-mannered man.

"And," he continued, "you're just the one who can do that for me. You certainly know the gambling business and you were always a totally honest newsman. So what more could I ask for?"

Before we ended our lengthy luncheon meeting, we worked out the details. Bob wanted a "no-holds-barred" article once a week. I was agreeable to writing a column on the gambling industry so long as he made me one promise: that he would never edit something out of my columns to bow to political pressure or to placate an advertiser. I'd been down that road many years earlier with another publisher, who would add paragraphs to my columns to suit his agenda. He'd sometimes even take potshots at local politicians I didn't even know. The promise became very expensive for Bob Brown, but he never broke it.

Everything started out nicely with my column. I wrote it from deep within the industry, since the bosses and owners of the resorts had known and trusted me for so many years. The door of almost every top executive in the casino business was open to me and my column grew from weekly to semiweekly and, finally, to six days a week. The column was of interest to many residents of Las Vegas, since it was the first window they'd ever had into the gaming industry, which controlled the economy of southern Nevada.

The paper was gaining circulation, and Bob said that his casino advertising was growing in tandem. Among the *Valley Times'* resort advertisers was Argent Corporation, which was covering all the bases as its bosses were perpetrating the greatest scam ever to hit Nevada. I wasn't writing much about Argent at the time, other than certain incidents reported to me that could be corroborated. But unknown to me, the Argent interests wanted to solidify their position with the *Valley Times*. They'd increased their advertising schedule and signed a major contract with Bob Brown, who accepted it all at face value. He assumed they were impressed with his paper and wanted to help support it. But he learned their true motives quite soon.

About a month after my column debuted, I began receiving telephone calls from someone I've never been able to identify. Most of the calls were placed to my home, where I'd set up an office. The caller was a woman with a perfectly modulated telephone voice. She would call me, leave a message, and have me call her back at a pay phone somewhere in Las Vegas. By the type of information the woman gave me, I knew it had come from very deep within Argent's inner circle.

She fed me information on all sorts of lawbreaking activities, power struggles, hirings, firings, and other inside dope that only someone totally involved in the operation could know. At first, I was frustrated by the information, because there was no way I could personally verify what she was telling me. And I wouldn't use information unless I knew it to be true.

Finally, one afternoon she called and told me she had something I could check. She said that at 8:30 that night, a half-hour after the performance of *Lido de Paris* began in the main showroom, when it would be fairly quiet in the casino, Frank Rosenthal would show up. He'd walk through the pit area and fire various dealers, boxmen, floormen, pit bosses, and whomever else he planned to replace. She also told me that Rosenthal would have replacements lined up to step right in and take over the positions.

It all sounded ridiculous. No one would ever handle a wholesale discharge of employees in such a fashion. At least, I didn't think so until that night, when I watched the whole thing go down.

I got to the Stardust with a half-hour to spare and hid myself in the aisles of slot machines, not wanting to be seen or recognized by anyone who might alert Rosenthal. At exactly 8:30, Rosenthal appeared. He waved to a couple of people, then approached the pit. He consulted a piece of paper as he walked from table to table. He finally stopped at a blackjack table where no one was playing.

He said something to the male dealer, who immediately walked away, obviously dismayed. Rosenthal then waved his hand and held up some fingers, signaling to a crowd of people milling around the cashier's cage. A short heavyset young lady wearing a Stardust dealers uniform came waddling over and assumed her post at the table. I watched this scene repeated over and over, wondering what criteria he was using to replace this many experienced, and I assumed loyal, employees. I knew some of them had worked at the Stardust for 20 years or more.

It took an hour for Rosenthal to complete his task. Now there was a new crowd of uniformed dealers milling around the cashier's cage — the people he'd just fired. Rosenthal left the gaming area without even glancing over at them. He boarded the private elevator back to his lavish offices. One of his underlings came and dispersed the crowd, informing the dealers that their final paychecks were waiting for them in the timekeeper's office.

I rushed to the offices of the *Valley Times* and rewrote the lead item for my next column. I reported to the residents of Las Vegas what had been going on in their town the night before while they were busy watching prime-time

TV. The night became a part of Las Vegas history and is still known as the "Stardust Slaughter." That column item drew a lot of phone calls and mail to the paper and to me, congratulating the *Valley Times* as being the one paper in Las Vegas with the guts to report the "real news."

But the item also drew a threatening phone call from the Stardust's advertising director, who warned Brown that this type of coverage wouldn't be tolerated by the major advertiser. Bob never said a word to me, either about the Argent deal or the phone call.

From then on, I trusted my phantom lady caller, who would regularly stagger me with what she had to say. It became obvious that she either worked for or was related to someone who sat on the Argent board of directors. I finally narrowed the field to three of those insiders, but I've never been able to learn which one of them was so concerned about the terrible state of affairs that she was willing to risk everything, maybe even her life, by leaking such information.

A couple of weeks after I used the item on the wholesale firing, I got a phone call from a young woman who'd worked for me at Recrion and was now employed by Argent. She'd been instructed to deliver a message to me that essentially threatened my well-being if I continued to write "lies" about Argent. I copied her exact statement in a letter to my attorney, my wife, and my publisher. I detailed the situation and gave my personal analysis of what the thinly veiled threats actually meant and who was behind them. Then I sat down at the typewriter and wrote a column delineating my view of the kind of people who made such threats.

Less than a week later, someone who was well-connected informed me that the people in Chicago had read the column and made it clear to Lefty that if any physical harm happened to befall me, he would be held responsible. All was quiet from then on — at least where I was concerned. The Argent people continued to snipe at Bob Brown, however. His advertising contract was at stake, yet he remained stoic about it. Every time I hammered another nail into the Argent coffin, Bob Brown would commend me and enourage me to keep going. Had I known about the pressure under which he was living because of my writing, I would have done something to try to help him keep the paper afloat.

My column on the "Stardust Slaughter" prompted other people to come forward with dirt on Argent. The entire Argent mess was becoming laughable; I was being fed so much information from so many diverse sources that I was printing news from inside the organization before most of the Argent staff was even aware of it.

My sources continued to expand, even outside of Argent. Rosenthal had done such an excellent job of alienating people in the state that they all wanted to help nail him if they could. Someone had even made arrangements to fly a bundle of the *Valley Times* to Carson City each morning and place a paper on the desks of the governor, the attorney general, every member of the State Assembly and Senate, and all members of the Gaming Control Board and Gaming Commission. Things were getting hotter by the day.

Soon, Gaming Commissioners were calling me for information. The chairman, now U.S. Senator Harry Reid, became my friend as he pumped me for more details. He revealed that plenty of pressure was on state officials to at least remove Rosenthal from his position of authority at Argent. But I knew that one reason state officials weren't moving against Rosenthal was that some of them were on the Argent payroll. Many individuals within the various layers of government had taken money from Argent and they were fighting hard to maintain their payoffs.

I kept the heat turned up in my column.

Eventually, I was visited by a well-known attorney who invited me out to lunch. I had no reason to suspect that he was in any way connected with Argent, but it soon became obvious. I played dumb as he tried in every manner possible to make me a monetary offer in return for leaving Argent alone in my column. I wouldn't tumble and finally forced him to come out with the actual words. He wanted to know how much it would take for me to stop writing anything about Argent, period. Nothing good. Nothing bad. Nothing at all.

I contemplated his offer for a few moments, looked at him gravely and explained that every man has a price. And I was no different. I told him that if his clients would place a million dollars in a Swiss bank account for me, I would stop writing about Argent — or anyone else. In fact, I would retire immediately. We both had a good laugh.

Argent made one more pass at Bob Brown in an attempt to muzzle the column. Bob refused and they pulled all their advertising from his paper.

Bob Brown never recovered from the Argent ordeal. His problems were compounded by IRS claims that he owed back taxes on employee withholding. His financial situation was in desperate straits, as it had been so many times in his life. Knowing Bob, he could have pulled through and kept publishing the real news. But his heart gave out and he died of what they said was a heart attack. I felt then, as I still feel today, that Bob Brown died of a broken heart.

13

The Skim

Slot machines, today the very backbone of the profits for most Las Vegas casinos, were not always so welcome by the bosses. While slots kept the wives of the players amused and enabled guests waiting in lines to enter a restaurant or showroom to get rid of their spare change, they were considered a nuisance by most gambling operators. It was rare to find more than 25 or 30 of the one-armed bandits in any casino.

The machines, most of which took a single nickel at a time, paid back an average of 45 percent. At the Flamingo, one very large machine, known as a "Big Bertha," took a dollar at a time and paid a jackpot of $5,000. While today that amount would be considered a minor jackpot, in 1961 a $5,000 slot jackpot had even more impact than today's Megabucks' jackpots of $10 million or more.

One evening, the Big Bertha was hit for the $5,000 jackpot by a young couple from Ohio on their honeymoon. They were on their way into the showroom when they dropped a single silver dollar and struck the mother lode. They collected their winnings as quickly as possible, announcing that they were cutting their honeymoon short and returning to Ohio to use the cash as a down payment on a home. It was a very touching scene.

Knowing the newspapers in Ohio would publish this type of information, I gathered all the pertinent facts on the couple and wrote a story. It was carried around the world by all the major wire services.

Today casinos are forced to empty their machines two or three times daily, collecting a wash bucket full of coins each time from each machine. But back then slot machines got so little play that they were rarely opened more than once a week to collect the few coins. This particular Big Bertha dollar machine received so little play that no one bothered to open it, even after the jackpot was hit—until a month later, when the slot manager saw a story on the front page of the *Las Vegas Sun*.

There was our happy honeymooning couple trying to hide their faces behind handcuffed hands. On a table in front of them were a couple of packets of $20 bills in wrappers emblazoned with the Flamingo logo. The cute couple had been busted in a narcotics raid and the authorities were ready to investigate why Flamingo money bands were found at the scene. The slot manager immediately called a mechanic and they opened the back of the Big Bertha. Inside, they found that one of the paper reels, which held the fruit and jackpot symbols, was ripped and hanging off its wheel. Further inspection revealed that a tiny hole had been drilled through the side of the machine and strands of piano wire had been inserted to stop the reels in the jackpot positions. One of the wires had torn the paper.

That was when slot machine operators began beefing up measures to prevent cheating the machines. Of course, anything made by man can be figured out by man, and the cheats are still in business.

Today slot machines are the greatest thing in the world for casinos. First, they're minimally labor intensive. While it takes a crew of at least four employees to man a single crap table, those same four people (two change people, a floorman, and a mechanic) can easily handle as many as 60 slot machines. Also, security is much simpler. The employees have little contact with the cash, which goes directly into the machines. The machines are emptied by crews kept under close and continuous surveillance. How many heavy coins can an employee walk off with, anyway?

Oh, some scams are still out there, and they'll never end. If there's money laying around, you can bet there are plenty of individuals coming up with ways to get it. Cheats buy the first machines built in a new series. They study them, figure out all the electronics, then devise the means for beating them. Today's slot machine cheats are highly sophisticated computer experts, who devise their own computerized programs to take full advantage of any minuscule error or glitch that's exploitable.

Few slot machine cheaters, however, could even dream of coming anywhere close to the greatest slot machine scam in Nevada history. How about an estimated $15 million a year for five years? Yes, that amounts to some $75 million.

By 1974, when Rosenthal was calling the shots at the Stardust, the number of underworld-controlled resorts and casinos was being squeezed down by the feds, the state, and the corporations. Thus, fewer places that were still mob-controlled had to take care of more crime families throughout the country. Because the Chicago Mafia still held the reins on the Stardust and Fremont, money made at those hotels had to help support crime families that had been forced out of the Las Vegas picture. Chicago needed big bucks to go all around.

I had no idea how they'd get that much money without

showing it as income and paying state and federal taxes on it. But I'd been in the business long enough to know it would be done.

In the middle of the Argent situation, I was paid a visit by a pair of investigators from the Nevada Gaming Control Board, the enforcement agency in charge of ensuring the honesty of the casinos. They claimed to be investigating allegations that Argent was engaged in skimming. It was the first time I'd heard the astronomical sums they suspected were being forwarded to the hidden Chicago ownership untaxed. But they also admitted to me that the investigation was going nowhere.

I hit paydirt when I got a phone call from my mystery lady, who informed me that all the coins from all the slot machines at the Fremont and Hacienda were being taken to the Stardust slot-counting area. Then she let me in on the big secret.

In gambling's days of old, skimming cash off the top without reporting it was fairly widespread. But the situation was no worse than in almost every business in the country that handled cash. The Las Vegas and Reno casino operators got into trouble with the feds primarily because the government couldn't find other violations to hang on them. Failure to pay taxes was always a sure bet.

Of course, the real "take" was unknown—unless the perpetrators happened to get caught, as they did in the Flamingo situation. It had been only six or seven years since most of the top executives at the Flamingo got popped for skimming an annual $5 million. But as the Argent situation unwound, I could see the magnitude of the skim was far greater. For one thing, three casinos were involved in the Argent skim, including the Stardust, which was the busiest casino in Nevada at the time.

As it turned out, the Argent skim was the largest theft

from a Nevada casino ever reported. Those who put the scam together had it extremely well-planned.

The key to the take-off was the count. In major casinos the amount of money poured through slot machines results in such a huge volume of coins or tokens that counting it, even with high-speed machines, is impossible. Instead of counting, major casinos use ultra-sensitive scales to weigh the coins and determine their value; the scales are accurate down to a half-dozen or fewer coins. A portion of the coins is shunted into wrapping machines to be re-used within the casino, while the remainder is poured into bags and shipped to banks on a daily basis for deposit in the hotel's accounts.

But at the Stardust, things were handled differently. In a major breach of regulations, filled coin buckets were transported from Argent's other properties, the Fremont and Hacienda, to the Stardust for handling and counting. Once the coins arrived, they were taken to the hard-count room and dumped into hoppers atop the electronic scales.

Of course, the people at Argent preferred a less-than-exact calibration on the huge scales. They imported a mechanic who rewired the electronics so that when the weighed dollar coins were worth, say, a thousand dollars, they would actually register only nine hundred dollars. Once the bosses found how easy it was to do, they did the same thing with quarters.

The amount shown on the rigged scales was handled in the approved manner. The coins were rewrapped and used in the casino or bagged and shipped to the banks. The unreported coins were taken into the casino and brought to the same change booths where customers bought rolls of coin from hotel cashiers. In normal situations, change girls, who roam the casino and sell coin to players, also get their coins from the cashier. But there was a separate arrangement for the Stardust change girls. They got their coins from locked cabinets scattered around the casino floor. They placed their paper money in the repository slot and withdrew rolls of coins in the denominations needed.

The change girls knew nothing about the skim; they were simply following procedures set up by management. But the repositories were stocked with the unweighed coins by people in on the take. They'd refill the stands with untaxed coins on a daily basis and remove the currency at the same time. It was not unusual for a single change stand to have more than $10,000 a day in the illegal repository.

When you're talking about nickels, quarters, and dollar tokens, it's hard to fathom $15 million a year. However, when you realize that major casinos handle millions of dollars from their slot machines every day, the $15 million figure makes more sense. All the cash was turned over to the underworld with no taxes ever paid on it.

While the data necessary to make a case was being collected by the Control Board agents, the skim continued, as it did even after I began reporting the information I was getting from the state investigators and other sources. As testimony to just how brazen the Argent people were, during this same time period, Jay Vandermark—the slot department manager for the Stardust who'd been brought over from the Fremont by Rosenthal—was found murdered in Mazatlan, Mexico. Prior to joining Rosenthal at the Stardust, Vandermark had earned a reputation as a top-flight slot cheater and, according to my contacts, had designed the skimming program for Rosenthal. Needless to say, Vandermark's murder was never solved.

Through all the adverse publicity, the Control Board investigation, the heat from the honest state officials and the dissolution of his marriage, Frank Rosenthal remained the man in charge. He even had the audacity to star on his own television talk show, called the "Stardust Line." This was especially ironic, since Lefty had never applied for his gaming license. He maintained his proprietary position in the casino by assuming various other titles that didn't require a license. At one point he was the Stardust's director of food and beverage. Then he took the title of entertainment director. In fact, during the time I was serving as director of marketing, Rosenthal was using business cards that named him as *assistant* director of marketing. I learned this when federal investigators came to me and wanted to know what Rosenthal's job was while he was supposedly employed by my department!

Finally County Commissioner Bob Broadbent, a totally straight political leader with no personal axes to grind, made the suggestion that perhaps Clark County should hold its own hearing on the licensing of the Argent properties. Since casinos had to be licensed by both the state and the county where they operated, the county license, which was usually a rubber stamp of the state permit, could be used strategically in the Argent case.

Broadbent's threats, along with his personal visits to Rosenthal and other Argent officials, finally caused state authorities to force Rosenthal to appear for licensing. He was refused. In short order, the State Gaming Commission pulled the gaming licenses of the three Argent-owned-and-operated hotels—and they were out of business.

But that wasn't the end of the Stardust morass. Far from it.

14

The Heat Is Turned Off

Not too long after I was fired by Frank Rosenthal and while I was writing my six-day-a-week column for the *Valley Times*, I was offered a job as director of marketing by the Four Queens Hotel, the downtown resort that Ben Goffstein had built. I discussed my situation with David Hood, the CEO of the Four Queens, and Bob Brown. I explained to both my feeling that I'd never have a conflict of interest between my job at the hotel and the column. I knew the Four Queens was so squeaky clean that a controversy could never arise. And it was true. While I was employed there, David Hood passed away and I became a staunch supporter of, and aide to, his wife Jeanne, who became president of the Hyatt-owned hotel. I stayed at the Four Queens for about six years.

During that time, the feds continued their campaign to force the mob from the Las Vegas casino business. They'd gotten rid of the Dalitz organization at the Desert Inn, the Florida mobsters at the Flamingo, and the Rosenthal group at the Stardust. They were now launching investigations into various other casino properties.

Their primary targets became the Aladdin and the Tropicana where, they claimed, unsavory types held hidden ownership. When it became obvious that the ownership at the Tropicana would be forced out in favor of new clean buyers, I suggested that my employer, Hyatt Corporation, look into the situation. At the time, Hyatt held licenses for the Four Queens and the Hyatt Tahoe, on the north shore of Lake Tahoe in northern Nevada.

The Hyatt people were interested. Negotiations for the purchase proceeded smoothly until the day before Jay Pritzker, president of Hyatt Corporation, was supposed to arrive in Las Vegas, bearing a check as the binder for a deal. Hyatt's comptroller was visiting with one of the embattled Tropicana owners when the owner's secretary delivered a copy of the *Las Vegas Review-Journal*, which had just arrived. The comptroller happened to see the headline on page one, which told of more mob figures who were supposedly involved in the ownership web of the property. The money man excused himself and left.

Even though all the suspected mobsters would have been taken out of the operation by a Hyatt purchase, the corporate bosses decided to back away. Not long afterward, Ramada Corporation bought the Tropicana, then created Aztar Corporation. Since the Aztar takeover, the Tropicana has had its financial ups and downs, but its legal problems ended.

At the Aladdin, St. Louis attorney Sorkis Webbe held forth as chairman and majority shareholder in a property that had been marginal ever since it was first built in the early 1960s as a non-gaming hotel, the King's Crown Tally Ho. A lengthy list of owners had passed through since, and most of them left as losers.

Under Webbe's stewardship, the property attracted close scrutiny from federal authorities. There were hints of some unlicensed owners involved in the Aladdin, along with some large amounts of money finding its way from the Aladdin's coffers into the hands of questionable characters in Michigan. Finally federal indictments were issued, which gave the Nevada Gaming Commission the right to order the casino locked up until the criminal charges were disposed of, one way or another.

Harry Reid, still chairman of the Gaming Commission, contacted Webbe and Richard Daly, president of the Aladdin, suggesting that the owners voluntarily close the casino, rather than force the state to take such action and give Nevada gambling yet another black eye. When Reid was unable to work anything out with the hotel owners, he called me and proposed that I speak with Webbe and Daly.

"You have good connections there," Reid told me. "Maybe you can convince them of the great service it would be for them to send us a letter stating that they're voluntarily closing the casino until they can escape this cloud caused by the indictments."

I went to the Aladdin and met with Webbe and Daly. Our meeting continued through dinner as Webbe steadfastly refused to write the letter or make any such move on a voluntary basis. I told them there was little choice: If such a letter wasn't received by the Commission, there were plans for a forced closing at 4 p.m. the next day.

We haggled through the night and, at one point, the men agreed to go along with the Commission's request. A stenographer was called and a letter was formulated. However, Sorkis Webbe, the attorney, and Richard Daly, the businessman, kept disagreeing on the letter's exact wording.

Finally Webbe stormed out of the office, yelling that he was going for a cup of coffee. The stenographer quickly disappeared. Daly said he was giving up and going home. "It's up to Sorkis now," he shrugged. "If he doesn't mind the idea of the Gaming Control Board coming in and locking up the joint, so be it."

I still wasn't ready to give up, primarily because I didn't want to provide the national media with more fodder for yet another scandal in the Las Vegas gambling industry, in which I'd now spent the lion's share of my career. It was actually for these same reasons that I'd refused several offers to syndicate my gaming column to newspapers throughout the country. The idea of hanging Nevada's dirty laundry all over the place, of having people who knew almost nothing about the gambling business make determinations strictly from what I wrote, was distasteful to me. The subjects of my columns were a strictly local matter as far as I was concerned.

I went downstairs to the coffee shop, where I found Webbe seated by himself in a booth, grimly staring at a half cup of coffee. We chatted amiably and he leveled with me on some of his reasons for not wanting to write the requested letter. At about six in the morning, I made one final request and Webbe again declined. As we parted, I told him I'd be seeing him later in the day.

A few hours later, when Reid arrived at his office, I called him and advised him of what did not happen through the night. He then told me that representatives of the Gaming Control Board would arrive at the Aladdin at four that afternoon. They were right on time. They walked through the casino to the cashier's cage and delivered papers notifying all concerned that the casino was closed. Then they walked through the entire gaming area and asked guests and employees alike to leave the casino.

The gaming authorities began removing all the portable gaming equipment—playing cards, dice, even roulette wheels — and placing sealing tape on every slot machine. It was a sad time.

The Aladdin bosses were ultimately convicted on a variety of charges in federal court and the resort went through a string of ownerships and bankruptcies that lasted many years. As I write, the Aladdin has been imploded to make way for a new Aladdin, this one costing $600 million and boasting 3,000 rooms and a shopping mall.

The Stardust's Last Stand

In 1981, when Argent Corporation had its gaming licenses revoked at the Stardust, Fremont, and Hacienda hotel-casinos, Al Sachs, the former boss of Recrion Corporation and one of the nicest men I'd ever worked for, applied for permission to purchase the Stardust and Fremont. Harry Reid, still heading the Gaming Commission, knew I'd worked for Sachs and asked for a personal evaluation. Reid told me he'd never really gotten to know Sachs, but the FBI was putting tremendous pressure on the Gaming Commission not to license him, having pegged him as a front for the Chicago underworld.

I leveled with Reid when I told him that I believed Al Sachs was one of the best resort operators I'd ever known. However, I agreed that such a changeover could turn out to be cosmetic only, another inside sale to another sacrificial lamb for Chicago.

There was no other way I could explain the situation to the head of the Gaming Commission. However, I did tell Reid that, cosmetically, Sachs would be a tremendous improvement over the likes of Lefty Rosenthal, and there was a good chance the Chicago interests might back away from interfering in the operations, because of the notoriety heaped on them as the result of the Argent scandal.

Sachs was approved and he offered me my old job back. I grabbed the opportunity. Some nasty tales had been told about me and everyone else who'd been in the Recrion operation when Lefty Rosenthal and his crew moved in and got rid of us. I wanted an opportunity to vindicate myself. Sachs made it clear to me that his intentions were similar. He told me Chicago was leaving him alone and he'd be allowed to repair the damage caused by the Argent regime.

I then went to Bob Brown and explained that I'd be forced to stop writing the column. The Stardust and Fremont had been involved in too much controversy, much of which was caused by my own writings. The thought of reporting honestly on the gambling industry while being employed by properties that might get into jams seemed impossible.

Over Brown's objections, I left the newspaper business again. It was a wrenching situation. I knew, as Brown did, that my column had attracted a lot of attention to his new newspaper and helped increase his circulation and advertising sales. But I was hot to rejoin the industry I'd helped to shape and come to love.

Returning to my offices at the Stardust and getting reacquainted with staff members who'd survived the Argent regime and others who were also coming back to be with Sachs once again was a ball. The family was together again, working to restore the Stardust and Fremont to their former glory. And it stayed good for six months, almost to the day.

That's when I suddenly began seeing changes in the Sachs administration. This open friendly executive, who was as much a friend as an employer, suddenly became distant. He started taking trips and when he was at the hotel, he did everything possible to avoid his executive staff. At the same time, an individual whom Sachs had been previously forced by Chicago to keep on the staff was now back, participating more and more in operations. It quickly became obvious to me that Chicago had let the heat die down for half a year, but was now back in charge. I knew what was about to happen, and I knew it was going to be bad — again.

Joyce and I had already discussed the possibility of semi-retiring and now, with the handwriting on the wall, we started making serious plans. We put our home up for sale and contacted business brokers, seeking an opportunity that would take us far away from all of this.

I went to see Al Sachs and tendered my resignation, effective in 60 days. Sachs was shocked, but he confirmed my suspicions when he said quietly, "I only wish I could be going with you."

Neither of us said any more.

I often wonder if Sachs realized just how prophetic his words were. A few months later the Gaming Control Board and Gaming Commission came down hard on his corporation. Though the Chicago influence was now blatant, Sachs, true to form, accepted total responsibility for the new set of allegations, whether he even knew about them or not. He, too, lost his gaming license and the Chicago mob finally lost its control over the Stardust and Fremont hotels when the gaming authorities made it crystal clear that they would not allow another inside "sale." Both properties were bought by Boyd Gaming Corporation, a Las Vegas company owned and operated by a family of casino pioneers.

Leaving Las Vegas

It was difficult to pack up and leave the place that had become home to our entire family. The most difficult part was leaving the house we thought we'd keep for the rest of our lives. But situations change.

Some friends gave us a going-away party, where everyone made bets on how long we could stay away. The over/under was a year, with most people betting on the under. In January 1983, we left the resort-casino business and moved to what might as well have been a foreign country for us — rural New Hampshire — where we became the happy proprietors of a typical old country store in the town of Salisbury, population 750.

But before leaving Las Vegas, I wrote three final columns and gave them to Bob Brown. One was about the Las Vegas I had known. The second was about the Las Vegas I was leaving. And the third was a prediction of what Las Vegas would be 10 years after my departure.

All went smoothly when Bob published the first two columns. But when he printed my prognostication, it caused quite a controversy. I received telephone calls from casino bosses all over town who were angry and upset with my outrageous forecast: that slot machine play would surpass the action at the tables within 10 years.

My rationale was that, with more and more public corporations coming onto the scene, slot machines would appeal most to them. My guesstimate was actually wrong, however. It didn't take 10 years. It was less than three years later that the high-powered slot machines became more profitable than table games like craps, blackjack, and roulette. Casinos actually started removing many of their table games to clear more space for slot machines.

We stayed in New Hampshire for three years, until I

broke a leg falling off a ladder. This was right around the time that our real-estate broker brought us a buyer for our store who was willing to pay almost double what we'd bought it for. Of course we sold, and that's when our gypsy escapades began in earnest.

Our children were grown and we had plenty of money to retire. But we weren't exactly ready to move to Florida and play shuffleboard for the rest of our lives. I was then about 53 and still wanted to work. I considered buying a business outside of the gambling industry in Las Vegas, but Joyce wouldn't stand for that. She was afraid I'd be right back in the middle of things. We tried Reno for a while, then went back to New England, then wound up back in Las Vegas. I wanted to do some part-time work, but found that while we'd been away, I'd become something of a dinosaur in the resort-casino industry. I didn't know most of the executives in the business, and those I did know had surrounded themselves with the bright young spirits who are going to save Las Vegas.

Thinking of myself as a dinosaur gave me a new perspective on the town to which I'd devoted most of my life. It got me thinking about the "old days" and exactly when they ended. No doubt everyone would agree that Ben Siegel was assassinated in the old days and Kirk Kerkorian's 5,005-room MGM Grand is a product of the "new Las Vegas."

But if you ask when Howard Hughes was active in Las Vegas, or when Jackie Gaughan amassed his many casinos, or even when Steve Wynn came on the scene, the dates are a lot less distinct and the eras are much harder to pin down.

The modern history of Las Vegas, technically, dates back to 1931, the year the state of Nevada legalized wide-open gambling. Some old-timers cite 1950, the year the Desert Inn opened and triggered a building boom in Las Vegas, as the turning point at which the old ended and the new began. Still others point to 1966, when Howard Hughes showed up, swept away the mob era with his $300 million broom, and paved the way for publicly owned corporations to take over the town.

But I believe that the years prior to 1970 would be the "good old (bad old) days" and the years following would be the new era. It was in 1970 that the first public corporation (Hilton) bought its first hotel-casino (the Flamingo). The corporations weren't versed in the gambling business. It bears repeating that they thought they were buying resorts that happened to have casinos attached, when what they were really buying were casinos that happened to have hotel rooms, restaurants, and showrooms attached.

They quickly learned that the Las Vegas properties had to be handled differently than any other resort-hotels they'd ever operated. In Las Vegas, the rooms, food, entertainment, and other amenities were expected to lose money in order to entice the visitors to make up the difference in the highly profitable casinos. The new managers knew they had to instill sound business practices and profitability in all areas of their operations. They also wanted to distance themselves from the modus operandi of the old-school casino executives. While they learned important lessons about the casino business from the veterans, attrition and differences of opinion weeded out the old-timers and made room for the new breed of bosses.

I've always considered the 20 years from 1970 to 1990 as a transition period in Las Vegas. It took about that long for those now in control of the huge casino corporations to change the casinos-with-rooms into resorts-with-casinos.

Because the changeover was completed less than 10 years ago, the new Las Vegas is still a toddler. It will be learning for many years. Some of the lessons may be ones that were standard procedure from earlier days in the gaming industry. Others will be so new that they can barely be imagined even today. But to refer to the old days as categorically "good" and the new days as "bad" is as ridiculous as viewing it exactly the opposite.

Anyway, after a couple of years of hanging around while the new Las Vegas got its legs, we picked up stakes again and returned to southern California, where I went to work for one of our closest friends, a highly successful automobile dealer. Then, in 1994, we saw a classified ad in the *L.A. Times*. The owners of a 64-room resort in Big Bear Lake were looking for a couple to take over management of their property. We hit it off with the owners and took the job when it was offered to us.

Today I watch the action in Las Vegas with an interest that's a bit more detached. We're a fast 200-mile drive to the city and we still visit frequently to see family and friends, and to attend funerals. I still try to keep tabs on what might be happening in town, and periodically I send guest columns along to my old friend, Chuck Di Rocco, for use in his publication *Gaming Today*. I'm still trying to learn to accept the drastic changes that have taken place in the past decade or so. Any opinions I might have on Las Vegas as it is operated today must be considered "graveyard." Maybe someday this old fly on the wall will be able to discuss those views.

Epilogue

Friends, colleagues, and associates, both in and out of the gaming industry, asked why I didn't include tales about various other famous names in Las Vegas history. For example, because I worked at the Flamingo, which became the most infamous of Las Vegas resorts when Benjamin Siegel was murdered, they can't understand why I didn't go deeper into the Siegel era.

Siegel opened the Flamingo and was taken out during my final year of junior high school. Anything I might have written about Siegel or the Flamingo in those early days would have been hearsay. Hearsay was what I did my best to avoid in writing *Fly On the Wall*.

I wrote about people and events I knew from first-hand involvement. In almost every instance, I was there, participating, when the situation occurred.

A few of the true Las Vegas pioneers I'd have enjoyed writing more about include men like Sam Boyd, a wild success with his downtown casinos; Joe Kelley, who made the Showboat into the very first "neighborhood casino" by building away from both the Strip and downtown; Joe

Rosenberg, a true gentleman and a most capable casino owner and executive at the Flamingo and Riviera; Major Riddle, who helped turn the Hacienda into a big success, then moved to the struggling Dunes, which he made one of the most successful properties in Vegas; Harley Harmon, businessman and political leader, who was always able to keep the gamblers happy with Las Vegas and Las Vegas happy with the gamblers; E. Parry Thomas, the first banker to make loans to the casino industry; and Jerry Zarowitz and his close associate Elliott Price, the two men who really put the Caesars Palace dream together. Governors Paul Laxalt, Grant Sawyer, Mike O'Callaghan, and Richard Bryan, along with Gaming Commission chairmen Peter Echeverria and Harry Reid, were all good friends.

There are scores of others. The primary reason I omitted most of them is because I either judged their exploits to be of lesser interest to the reader or I didn't have a close enough relationship to get stories about them right.

I would like to cite Ken Frogley, who founded what was then known as the Desert Sea News Bureau, later renamed the Las Vegas News Bureau. Under Frogley and his successors, Jim Deitch and Don Payne, the Las Vegas News Bureau provided the world with the Las Vegas story, helping to make the city what it is today.

And then, of course, there is the "new breed," made up of Harvard Business School grads and other whiz kids. It's difficult to judge their accomplishments yet. They came to Las Vegas after others had worked so hard to develop the entire package. In my opinion, the newcomers and corporate types are still just holding on to the rocket that has been ascending for 40 years or more.

But I'll keep watching them. And if the good or the bad they might do for Las Vegas ever becomes evident, I'll report it to you.

Index

no image

About Huntington Press

Huntington Press is a Las Vegas-based book publisher. To receive a copy of the Huntington Press catalog, call 1-800-244-2224 or write to the address below.

Huntington Press
3687 South Procyon Avenue
Las Vegas, Nevada 89103
(702) 252-0655 • fax: (702) 252-0675
email: books@huntingtonpress.com

About The Author

Dick Odessky was a newspaperman in Los Angeles before moving to Las Vegas to ply his trade in the early 1950s. Later, he worked as a publicist and marketing director at several hotel-casinos. He lives with his wife in Big Bear Lake, California.

Author and jacket photo by Jason Cox
Jacket design by Jason Cox, Bethany Coffey and Laurie Shaw